YOU SUCK AT DRINKING

BEING A COMPLETE GUIDE TO DRINKING FOR ANY AND ALL SITUATIONS IN YOUR LIFE, INCLUDING BUT NOT LIMITED TO OFFICE HOLIDAY PARTIES, WEDDINGS, BREAKUPS AND OTHER SAD TIMES, OUTDOOR CHORES LIKE DECK-BUILDING, AND WHILE IN PUBLIC, LEGALLY AND ILLEGALLY

BY MATTHEW LATKIEWICZ

RUNNING PRESS
PHILADELPHIA · LONDON

Books published by Running Press are available at special discounts for bulk
purchases in the United States by corporations, institutions, and other organizations.
For more information, please contact the Special Markets Department at the Perseus
Books Group, 2300 Chestnut Street, Suite 200, Philadelphia, PA 19103, or call (800)
810-4145, ext. 5000, or e-mail special.markets@perseusbooks.com.

A portion of this book's material originally appeared in the "Sloshed" column on
grubstreet. com, *New York Magazine*'s Food and Restaurant Blog.

ISBN 978-0-7624-5104-3
Library of Congress Control Number: 2014953792

E-book ISBN 978-0-7624-5188-3

9   8   7   6   5   4   3   2   1
Digit on the right indicates the number of this printing

Cover and Interior design by Joshua McDonnell
Interior Illustrations by Carl Wiens
Edited by Jennifer Kasius
Typography: Avenir, Archer, SansSerif

Running Press Book Publishers
2300 Chestnut Street
Philadelphia, PA 19103-4371

Visit us on the web!
www.runningpress.com

CONTENTS

INTRODUCTION

First, let me raise my glass and say an opening prayer: **Cheers!** Now, we may begin.

The problem—one of them, at least—is that most of us were never taught what or how to drink, not really, not unless you count watching your uncles down dirty martinis, or high school football players shotgun beers, or overhearing waiters advise your parents on wine-food pairings at fancy restaurants. That education, while helpful, will only get you so far. Drinking is complicated, which is to say that it is simple, but because it makes you dumb and clumsy, it *feels* complicated.

Add to this that booze goes hand-in-hand with many different types of human endeavors. We drink to socialize, to celebrate, to drown sorrows; we drink in large groups, in small groups, and while alone; we drink on vacation, during work, and while we eat; we drink inside and we drink outside; we sometimes drink a lot and sometimes just a little. And yet while all these different scenarios require different drinking mentalities, our under-education means that, most of the time, we are ill-equipped to know what type is needed when and where.

Well, no more! To help you navigate your drinking life, I humbly offer this book, *You Suck at Drinking; Being a complete guide to drinking for any and all situations in your life, including but not limited to office holiday parties, weddings, breakups, and other sad times, outdoor chores like deck-building, and while in public, legally and illegally.* For instance: Have you ever wondered whether you can order a drink at lunch with your boss? Have you ever felt intimidated by a bartender? Or drunk too much at a wedding? Have you pretended to know more about wine than you actually do? Or gotten caught drinking a beer in public? Or jeez, have you ever drunk with your coworkers and made a pass at someone you *really* should not have made a pass at? There are many decisions about *what* and *how* to drink that depend on *when* and *where* and *with whom* you are drinking, decisions made all the more difficult because, well, you are drinking. Fortunately, the strategies and correct answers to these questions are all contained in this book.

• • •

I have been giving advice on drinking for over ten years, first as the owner of a café that served beer and wine in the fabled land of Montague, Massachusetts, and then in the international waters of the Internet and magazines as a drinks writer for such publications as *McSweeney's*, Grub Street, and *Details*. The book you hold in your hands is the knowledge culled from those years of experience, containing tongue-in-cheek advice, thoughtful reflection, and irreverent commentary—all in celebration of drinking.

Please note: I am not a bartender. This book will not provide recipes. I am also not a chef. This book will not instruct you on the intricacies of flavor and/or pairing your drink with food. I am, for better or worse (probably worse), a Drinker who writes about drinking. My research has been extensive, mostly accidental, often shameful. What I can teach you about drinking is probably not healthy or helpful in a life-goal-achieving sort of way. But we both know that you are going to drink and that you will make many mistakes along the way. So you may as well read this book and perform your drinking with as much care, attention, and forethought as when you play with your kids or do your taxes or whatever.

You Suck at Drinking is not so much a guide to alcohol as it is a guide to practicing good Drinkcraft. Will it prepare you to be the maid of honor at a wedding? It will. Will you learn how to drink to your advantage in casinos? You bet you will! What about children's birthday parties? Let me put it this way: all possible parties, *including* child-centric ones, will be explored.

Give this book to a college graduate, to new hires, to the person with whom you are becoming romantically involved. Let them learn from the mistakes and hard-won wisdom of those who have come before them, from those who have learned how to handle their liquor. This is the book that folks should be given on that fateful day when they take their first drink; the book that will steer them correctly away from the siren call of flavored vodka that awaits many of those who drink—but who are not yet *Drinkers*.

_____

DRINKER
CERTIFICATE

_____

This is to certify that _____

_of_ _____ _State of_ _____

Age _____ _Height_ _____ _Weight_ _____

is a regular at _____

With a bar stool placed _____

Favorite Cocktail _____

Hangover Technique _____

_____

Part 1:
TAXONOMY OF DRINK

It is not an easy job, learning your liquors, but Drinkers don't just drink what's easy. They drink what is available. To best navigate the world of liquor, a Drinker should be able to identify and classify any booze they may encounter. As you know, we humans evaluate the world through our *five senses*—sight, touch, smell, taste, and how drunk it makes us. All any young Drinker needs for liquor study is a faculty for using these senses, a notebook, and a sense of adventure.

When encountering a new liquor, an aspiring Drinker should approach it openly and with a respectful sense of caution. While it is true that trying some liquors for the first time can turn out bad—in that they either taste like or actually *are* Ouzo—others can turn out lovely, like maraschino or bourbon. You'll never know if you don't try! I always recommend that young drinkers scan a cocktail menu for drinks containing ingredients they have never heard of. This simple technique will acquaint you with most alcohols, especially if you live in a drinking city like San Francisco, New York, or any town in Louisiana.

Getting to Know Booze in Five Easy Steps

STEP 1: SEE

It has been said that, before you taste with your mouth, you should taste with your eyes. This is absurd. Never put alcohol in your eyes. In addition to making you blind drunk, your eyeballs actually have zero taste buds—you won't taste *anything*.

Liquor is consumed just like other liquid beverages.[1] If this is unfamiliar to you, I recommend you read my previous book, *The Mechanics of Drinking: A Primer on Consuming Liquid Beverages* before proceeding further.

When trying a particular liquor for the first time, take note of its bottle. You can tell a lot about what you are about to consume simply by how it is packaged **(see next page)**.

---

1   There are other nonstandard ways to drink liquor, true. Though not recommended for most situations, I've included them for the truly adventurous. See the table on Nonstandard and Mostly Made-up Ways to Consume Alcohol , page 26.

It's Easy to Identify
Liquor by the Label!

Anything at all pirate-related—pictures of pirates, of course, a label made to look like a treasure map, skull and crossbones, the word *Pacific* written in a pirate-y way.

This is rum.

Illustrations of British admirals—anything particularly colonial.

This is gin.

The bottle is a mason jar.

This is moonshine.

A hand-drawn picture of a fancy house and way more words than seem necessary.

This is wine.

The bottle is shaped like a stiletto high heel.

This is vodka.

The bottle is shaped like an Aunt Jemima bottle.

This is Frangelico.

The label makes you feel sick and turn away.

This is either Jose Cuervo or Jack Daniel's—or whatever you drank way too much of at one point, teaching you about hangovers.

The bottle comes in a weird cardboard tube, and old men hold it reverently.

This is Scotch.

The label mentions barrel aging, but doesn't have a picture of a fancy house on it.

This is bourbon.

The label has one of these things: a picture of Vermont, an illustration of a beard, a strong color correlation to the American flag, or anything vaguely monastic.

This is beer.

The label reads Jameson.

This is Irish whiskey.

The label reads After Shock.

Stay away.

STEP 2: TOUCH

You cannot consume alcohol without putting it into your mouth. How is this done? Through the magic of touch, of course! Grabbing a drink is one of the first ways to assert your drinking personality. Some popular Drink Grips are as follows:

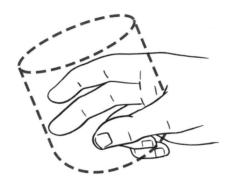

- The Classic C: Best for tumblers and cans.

- The Three-Finger C: A modified grip best for wine glasses and cocktail glasses.

- Alms for the Poor: Turn your hand palm up and set the glass in it. Only to be used when swirling Brandy in a smoking jacket.

- The Noose: A loose, laconic grip for beer bottles.

- The No-Hands: When you leave the drink on the bar and bring your face to it. Only to be used when a drink is too full or comes with a straw.

STEP 3: SMELL (OPTIONAL)

Your nose can be useful in determining whether a beverage in front of you contains alcohol or not. If you aren't sure, you should probably leave it be.

STEP 4: TASTE

Like coffee and the movies of Jim Jarmusch, alcohol is an *acquired* taste. Many people do not like the taste of alcohol at first. "Why would anyone drink this?" they think. And then they get drunk, and it becomes very clear why anyone–*including themselves*–would drink it. The taste of alcohol is great for many reasons, sure, but mostly it is great because it portends inebriation. Thus, when trying new alcohols, do not judge the flavor until you have become drunk from it. Remember, nothing tastes as good as being drunk!

What's the Proof?

||||||||||||||||||||||||||||||||||||||||||||||||||||||||||||||||||||||||||||||||||||||||||||||||||||||||||||||||||||||||||||||||||||||||

The proof of an alcohol describes the amount of ethanol in it. Ethanol is the chemical in booze that makes your brain work funny.[2] Like a lot of measurements made up by the British (yards, miles) "Proof" is strange and arbitrary and originally meant, "7/4 times the alcohol by volume (ABV)." I can't even begin to wrap my head around that, but now it is defined as twice the percentage of ABV. So, for instance, something that is 80 proof is 40% ABV, meaning that 40% of the liquor in front of you is pure ethanol. The higher the proof (or ABV) the more impact it has, obviously.

Interestingly, proof only refers to the hard stuff. You usually just say the percentage there. So, wine is usually around 12–14% ABV; beer can range, but the most common would be around 5–6%. Your spirits are gonna start at 40%, which would be, as we know: 80 Proof.

STEP 5: HEAR;
OR HOW DRUNK DOES THIS MAKE YOU?

Some liquors are stronger than others, and it is important that you assess the inebriation effects of your different alcohols so you can imbibe them properly. A shot of Chartreuse (120 proof) is not always appropriate, no matter how wonderful it may taste!

But how do you assess drunkenness? Use your hearing. Are sounds both loud and muffled at the same time? Like you are listening to something under water, but also, you have super-sensitive hearing like a bat? If so, whatever you just drank is pretty strong.

---

2   Ethanol is produced through the processes of fermentation and then distillation, which I am not going to explain because: Internet.

Because it can be hard to remember the details of what you drank while drinking, I recommend that you carry a small notebook so that you can keep a drinking log.[3] Drinking logs can take many forms, but I have provided a good template for the kind of information you should capture in order to imprint the new liquor into your memory.

```
Location _____

Date _____ Hour _____

Inebriation  1  2  3  4  5  6  7  8  9  10
.................................................................

        Sketch bottle - note any important
        markings on the label or otherwise
```

Feel free to copy this to make your own booklet. Leave the back side blank for any notes and/or drawings of cats or superhero insignias you feel compelled to add. Keep this booklet with you at all times. It will be a great reference when reading any cocktail menu or browsing any liquor store. You can know for sure if you have tried it and whether it tasted like (or was) Ouzo. I find myself browsing my drinking log even when not drinking—such as while jogging or at the dentist—simply to remind myself of the adventures I have had.

---

3   Many people are unaware that the poems of Charles Bukowski (a Drinker if there ever was one) are actually his drinking logs, i.e., descriptions of new liquors he tried.

While trying new adult beverages, it can be helpful to understand where each fits within the larger scheme of alcohol. Much like human families and NCAA March Madness contenders, all liquors can be organized into a tree-based diagram.

BOOZE

Made with care and precision and helpful when making cocktails

Unreal horrors marketed to young people

Cinnamon-flavored

Liquids you would describe as being "brightly colored"

Fortified Alcohol (e.g. Liqueurs and Fortified Wines)

Lawnmower beer

Beer beer

Nerdy beer

Stupid beer

Beer

Labeled "best value" according to a magazine you don't read

Kangaroos or sandals on the label

Cheap

Purchased for dinner party

Expensive

Good for picnics

Wine

Cough medicine

Anything with a screw cap

Spirits

- Vodka
  - Ripping you off vodka
    - Comes in a frosted glass bottle
    - Sounds Russian but is not made in Russia
  - Flavored vodka
  - Respectable enough
- Gin
  - Plastic jug gin
  - That British guy in the red coat and funny hat gin
  - The one with the cucumbers
  - The kind for people who say "Martinis are only made with gin"
- Whiskey
  - Irish Whiskey
    - Jameson
    - Wait, there's another Irish whiskey?
    - Probably, but no one has ever had it
  - Scotch
    - Campfire-flavored and given to you as a present from someone who plays golf
    - Campfire-flavored and too expensive for you
  - Bourbon
    - Jack Daniel's and Jim Beam
    - The kind made by young men with great haircuts and expensive jeans
  - Canadian whiskey
    - The ones Americans know about
    - The ones Americans don't know about
  - White whiskey
    - Legal and made in Brooklyn
    - Illegal and made in New Hampshire
- Tequila
  - Made you throw up once
  - Given to you by someone who uses the phrase "sipping tequila" unironically
- Rum
  - Pirate guy rum
  - Bat logo rum
  - Eggnog rum
- Brandy
  - The kind consumed by Hip-Hop Artists (e.g. "From the Bottle")
  - The kind consumed by rich men in robes

21

Alcohol is consumed through the
mouth in a ritual called *drinking*.

Standard Ways to Drink Alcohol, Still in Use Today

TERM	DESCRIPTION	PROMINENT USAGES
Neat	Just alcohol; no ice, no mixing, no stirring or shaking. Take the bottle and pour some into a glass. Refers only to spirits. While wine and beer are drunk this way, they do not require the specification, as it is assumed you will be drinking it neat. Unless you are drinking a wine spritzer, of course, which you serve on the rocks at a picnic in a magazine shoot.	Whiskey and brandy are often drunk neat. In Russia, vodka is drunk this way.
On the Rocks	Any alcoholic drink served over ice. Could be straight liquor or a cocktail.	Ice is used to mellow and even out the drink or to keep it really cold. Some drinks—especially summer ones—are always served on the rocks: Tom Collins, gin and tonic, mojito. Some drinks, like the margarita and the Negroni, swing both ways (ice or no ice), depending on the circumstance.

TERM	DESCRIPTION	PROMINENT USAGES
Straight Up	A cocktail shaken or stirred with ice to chill it, but then strained into a separate glass to create a drink is served without ice.	Many cocktails are served straight up–the martini, the sidecar, the Manhattan. Drinks that need no mellowing or would be weird if watered down.
Shot	A small amount of liquor–usually 1.5 ounces–served in a small glass and meant to be consumed quickly, or even all at once. Can either be a single liquor served neat, or a mixed drink.	Tequila and whiskey are common shots. There is a whole sub-drinking-culture of mixed-drink shots, which the author does not condone but which involve bad double entendres and even worse liquor combinations. For some reason, 90 percent of these involve Baileys Irish Cream or some type of schnapps.
As a Back	A small drink, not always alcoholic, meant to follow another drink, often a shot. The "back" counteracts–or washes away–the burn of the first drink in many cases, though it can also just be a nice way to order two drinks at once.	Juices often follow shots–"Can I get a tequila shot with a pineapple back?" Beer Is often served as a back to whiskey–"Can I get a shot and a beer back?" Pickle juice has recently been served as a back to whiskey because people like weird things–"Can I get a pickle back?"

TERM	DESCRIPTION	PROMINENT USAGES
Cocktail	Generic term for an alcoholic drink made by mixing two or more liquids together, at least one of which is alcoholic.	Any number of good cocktail manuals can be found with 1,001 cocktail recipes. For the serious Drinker, I recommend immediate familiarity with the martini, the Manhattan, the old-fashioned, the Negroni, and the sazerac.
Mocktail	Anything with Virgin in the name; anything with a stupid pun in the title; anything named for child movie stars from the 1930s; oh, right, and it's non-alcoholic and for kids.	Don't. Just . . . don't. You are an adult.
Punch	The oldest type of mixed drink, originally made with five ingredients: alcohol, sugar, lemon, water, and tea or spices. As with most things we associate with England, the recipe was brought over from India in the early seventeenth century. It is most often served communally—and, at fraternity parties, from a garbage can.	In the modern era, these are most often served in the daytime at outdoor parties, the details and color scheme of which originate from an issue of *Martha Stewart Living*.
Highball	One spirit mixed with a non-alcoholic soda or juice in a tall glass with ice. A simplified mixed drink made popular in the 1950s when people drank a lot, but couldn't be bothered to make complex drinks.	Tom Collins, Cuba libre; all the "and" drinks: gin and tonic, rum and Coke, whiskey and soda, gin and juice.

Shaking vs. Stirring

||||||||||||||||||||||||||||||||||||||||||||||||||||||||||||||||||||||||||||||||||||||||||||||||||||||||||||||||||||||||||||||||||||||||||||||||||||||||||||||||||

What is the best way to combine the ingredients of a cocktail—stirring or shaking? It's an age-old debate. Here are some general guidelines:

- You shake when there are non-alcoholic ingredients of different consistency that need help mixing with others: citrus, cream, eggs.

- You stir when you are dealing with an all-alcohol concoction. They will mix just fine without shaking because they are essentially the same consistency and weight. In fact, stirring is mostly about making the ingredients cold.

- Some other options:

- You build (i.e., you just pour one ingredient on top of the other in the glass) when using soda—because shaking soda would create a mess, and all soda drinks are served over ice so you don't need to stir them in order to make them cold.

- You stop, drop, and roll when your ingredients are on fire.

- You shake, rattle, and roll when trying to combine guitars, bass, and drums into a cocktail.

Nonstandard and Mostly Made-up Ways to Consume Alcohol

TERM	DESCRIPTION	USE IT IN A SENTENCE
Booze Luge	Some enterprising young college student tunnels out a block of ice. Liquor is poured at the top so that it runs through the ice tunnel (getting chilled in the process) and comes out at the bottom, where an enterprising young person waits, mouth open, to receive this very cold liquor.	"Dude, booze luge. Dude! DUDE!"
From Mama Bird	A drink mixed directly in the mouth of the bartender or host and then spit into your mouth.	"A margarita please, from mama bird."
The Snorkel	Prepared in the traditional way, but served down a snorkel. Note: Usually requires drinker to provide snorkel.	"Through the SNNNOOOORKELLLLL!"
On the Dirt	Drunk while on the back of a motocross bike during a race.	"Yo, brah, I'll take that sidecar on the dirt, if you don't mind."
On the Rock	A very expensive preparation in which both the bartender and the patron travel to Alcatraz for drink preparation and consumption. Be warned, however, that in some bars, ordering a drink this way will result in the patron forced to take a body shot off of professional wrestler Dwayne "The Rock" Johnson.	"May I get that martini up and with a twist and served on the rock? No, no, not the wrestler. Thank you."

Part II:
DRINKCRAFT

One of the hardest things Drinkers must learn is how to adapt their drinking to any given scenario in which they might find themselves. It is also one of the most rewarding and useful skills a Drinker may develop. Unlike pursuits like amateur surgery or ham radio operation, drinking can happen anytime, anywhere. It is important that you, as a Drinker, are prepared!

The perils are many. Wrongful drinking can lead to:

- Poor use of accents

- Inappropriate and/or amorous advances

- Social embarrassment

- Strange food choices

- Unwelcome merriment

- Random crying

- Stoop sleeping

- Unsuccessful feats of strength, like arm wrestling

You might look at the above list and think, "It is not worth it! Perhaps I will simply become a tea drinker!"

To which I say: Tea!? *TEA?!* Reader, I have never once drunk "tea," and I do not consort with those who do. Sure, tea may never lead to the unwelcome scenarios detailed above, but then tea is only ever consumed in grandparents' parlor rooms and depressingly quiet cafés. No one has consumed tea and then tried to ride a skateboard down the stairs! Tea has never inspired a love song or *any* song for that matter, besides those written about soft textures and blankets. The risks of wrongful drinking are there—oh, they are there!—but they are worth the rewards of successful drinking.

Success is within reach for all young Drinkers, *if they learn the skills detailed in this section.* You must be part detective, part adventurer, part performer. Several things should be kept in mind when going out drinking: First, plan your outfit, especially where jackets and bags are concerned. *A successful Drinker is one who still has his or her house keys at the end of the night.* Many a night, Drinkers return home only to realize that they must break into their own houses. Always keep your keys in physical contact with your body!

Second, know your role among your drinking companions. Are you the best friend? The coworker? The depressed and dumped mess? Each of these scenarios requires a different drinking strategy. I wish I could tell you that drinking as much as you can would be the correct approach in every situation, but it is not true. Things change with every occasion—drinking at a wedding is quite different than drinking at dinner with your boss—and depending on the role you are playing: the best friend must drink differently than the coworker, and so on.

Third, it doesn't matter what you like or don't like. Successful drinking is not about your tastes, but about your decisions. You may despise drinks made with rum, but if you find yourself at a pirate bar, it is the only appropriate choice.[4]

And lastly: It can be hard to dial in, but get to know the difference between too drunk and not drunk enough.

---

4   But please don't wear an eye patch if you don't need one. That is just rude.

While every day will bring new challenges and opportunities for a Drinker, a daily drinking routine can help establish good patterns and appropriate inebriation that are as beneficial as any exercise routine. What should you drink at 11 a.m., for instance? How inebriated should you be at 3 p.m., and then at 3 a.m.? Answers to these questions—and more—can be found in the following chart. While just a guideline, it can help you make decisions that are right for you and right for drinking.

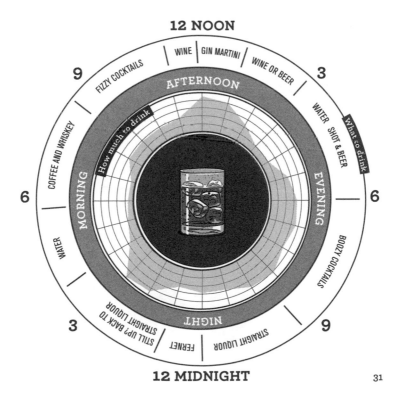

DRINKING AND YOUR DEVICES

There was a time when drunk people could safely attempt ill-advised feats of strength, propose marriage to a bush, and/ or tell their best friend that yes, they did indeed lose their shirt somewhere, but come on, they are *not that drunk*—all without anybody really remembering it, including themselves. We no longer have that blissful forgetfulness. Whether it's 3-a.m. drunk texts to ex-boyfriends, photos of you climbing a streetlamp that someone else posts on Instagram, or video of yourself taken accidentally while trying to turn on the flashlight app to find your keys on the bar floor, cell phones capture our drunken embarrassments and have the potential to keep them around forever.

To help us keep our drunken antics from going viral, I have developed this Drinking and Devices Safety Sheet.

STOP

This phone is OUT OF ORDER until tomorrow morning when you can figure out how to operate tape again.

Sincerely,

Your earlier, smarter self.

P.S.: Check your pockets. Still got your keys?

Cut it out and tape it over the screen of your phone as you order your first drink.

Any adult who desires to become a Drinker will want to develop a good rapport with our special friends, the bartenders. Even dull people can benefit from learning the basics about our "stewards of the sauce." Ordering a drink can be a stressful and perplexing affair, but with just a bit of study, Drinkers will find themselves calm and collected no matter who is standing behind that bar.

Waxed Mustache

Description: Resemble photos and etchings of bartenders from the nineteenth century. Common accessories include apron, arm garters, and possibly—in extreme cases—a bowler hat.

Environment: Originally found behind the unmarked doors and basements of the late 1990s neo-speakeasies, the "waxed mustache" migrated aboveground as a result of the great classic-cocktail pandemic of the early 2000s. However, they can only survive in environments with fresh juices and syrups.

How to treat them: Let them lead in this dance. Ask their advice, and don't presume to be the expert. This will only spook them. This bartender can be a great guide into the more obscure spirits and techniques, so have a sense of adventure, and do not rush the experience.

A point on safety: Do not talk to these bartenders while they do their special double cocktail shaker thing. You wouldn't talk to a drummer mid-drum, would you? Exactly.

Motto: "I think you'll like this."

The Rocker

Description: Sleeveless, classic rock T-shirt; long hair, wispy facial hair; and/or a really serious tattoo situation. Clearly does not give a fuck.

Environment: Native to the roadside honky-tonk and motorcycle bar, this breed can also be found in dingy bars the world over.

How to treat them: Just because they act cooler than you does not mean they are cooler than you. It means that they are way cooler than you, and nothing you do is going to change that. Please do not comment on a Rocker's band shirt; it will not impress.

Wait until a Rocker points at you, order your drink quickly, and then pay for it. That is as far as this relationship is going to go.

Motto: A subtle nod in your direction.

The Matthau

Description: No one can lean on a bar with a towel over a shoulder quite like the Matthau. Older, usually with a paunch, though in the case of the female Matthau (also called the Rhea Perlman) the paunch is replaced with wild, tall-teased hair. Signature look is a glower. Signature move is slowly wiping out the inside of a glass.

Environment: The natural habitat is the small-town bar, though city-dwellers can often find one in older, often ethnic neighborhoods. The Matthau thrives in a slower-paced environment and has the force to actually slow the whole bar down to accommodate their plodding style. Often owners of their joints, they have an incredible, nearly sea turtle-length, life span.

How to treat: The birdsong of this bartender is "What'll it be?"—though don't take that to mean it can be whatever you want. The Matthau can only prepare a few items, most of which are pints of beer.

The rule of thumb here is to imagine the Matthau, himself, drinking what you are about to order. If you can't imagine it, don't order it. Which is not to say that this type of bartender is mean or unaccommodating, but like the sea turtle, it will take time before he or she gets to know you.

Motto: "What'll it be?"

The Fraternity Brother

Description: Backward baseball cap, striped polo shirt. Looks way too young to be serving drinks.

Environment: Also a dweller of college towns, the Fraternity Brother can be a Matthau in the making.

How to treat them: Treat similar to the Matthau, but with less reservation. Can be greeted with a complicated handshake/ slap combination.

Motto: "How we doing?" Also: "What's your poison?"

The Siren

Description: Prominent cleavage, short-shorts, navel exposed—and that is just the gay male version of this bartender. Whether male or female, the siren has evolved for one thing and one thing only: a sex appeal meant to increase the amount you drink and tip. Often wearing cowboy hats.

Environment: This breed thrives in the college town bar, though many other bars have brought in Sirens due to their profitability. You will find Siren bartenders wherever there is a high concentration of male patrons (gay and straight).

How to treat them: Try your best not to look a Siren in the eye . . . or the chest. Once this bartender has you in his or her sights, you may as well hand over all your money and prepare to wake up tomorrow hungover and alone . . . certainly not next to the Siren.

The actual ability to make drinks is unnecessary for Sirens, though they are excellent at pouring shots and working crazy fast. They are also one of the few breeds who can smoothly handle an order of "three Stellas, four shots of Patrón, two with pineapple backs, and your phone number."

Motto: "You can totally take this shot."

The Tom Cruise

Description: Similar to the Siren, but male, straight, and usually less good-looking. They compensate with crazy bottle tricks and Vegas-style swagger.

Environment: Because a large part of their behavior includes showmanship, Tom Cruises dwell almost exclusively in casinos and resort towns. Unless you are on a soulless and dystopian vacation, no bar-goer actually wants to wait through the ten minutes of bottle flipping and fire-breathing that it takes the Tom Cruise to make a gin and tonic or whatever.

How to treat them: Whereas the Siren almost denies your existence, the Tom Cruise craves it, which can be even more dangerous. You might get a drink, but at the cost of your time. The best strategy when ordering from a Tom Cruise is to back away slowly while he is balancing a bottle on his chin . . . and go find another bar.

Motto: "Hey ladies, can I make you a drink?" (Eyes full of desperate eagerness.)

The Yacht Club
(aka The Suburban Hotel)

Description: Wears a bow tie and vest worthy of any tux rental shop in town. Often quiet and clumsy, these are mostly new and seasonal bartenders just working the summer after their senior year in high school. Similar to the mayfly, they are weak and numerous. Many are legally able to make drinks but not consume them.

Environment: As the name implies, this breed is found in our wealthier gated communities—places with money but little taste.

How to treat them: Because these bartenders have often taken a three-day bartending course in a hotel conference room, they are some of the few who know how to make a Fuzzy Navel or a Long Comfortable Screw Up Against a Wall without having to look them up.

Not that you should order one of those drinks: no adult should be made to say the word *fuzzy* and *navel* in the same sentence. This is the only bartender interaction during which you hold all the power. Use that power for good and instruct Yacht Clubs in the finer points of some of our more simple, classic drinks: a Negroni or a Manhattan would be a welcome addition to their arsenal of drinks, most of which are named after drunken spring break activities.

Motto: "Oops, sorry about that."

The Shining

Description: What the Yacht Club bartender used to be, before his patrons needed to be "corrected." Usually named Lloyd.

Environment: Found in the fugue states of insane people.

How to treat them: If you are actually seeing a bartender named Lloyd who rolls his *r*'s, you need more than a drink because you are about to murder your family.

Motto: "Your money's no good here."

Parties of All Types: A Complete List

Drinking at parties is in many ways the most basic and fundamental type of drinking. It is definitely the most common, and it speaks to the main reason most folks drink in the first place: to have fun and loosen up among others.

This is not to say that drinking at parties is simple or cannot be improved. Too often have I seen an outdoor garden party (page 45) stocked solely with beer. Beer! Maybe for a backyard party (page 46)—*maybe*. But a garden party? Drinker, I am not ashamed to admit that I nearly whipped up a batch of mojitos, myself. Similarly, I have seen individuals imbibe *too much* at a weeknight get-together, and *not enough* at their own birthday party.

Party-based drinking fails so often because it *seems* so simple. But just as the simple rules of chess belie an extraordinarily complex game, successful party drinking requires both strategy and cunning. From a few basic precepts emerges an intricate and subtle universe.

How and why one drinks at a retirement party for a colleague you didn't particularly like is completely different from the hows and whys of drinking at a child's birthday party—*especially if that birthday party involves a clown*.

Once you know the party type, you can dial in your drinking.

Each party has an average inebriation level, a level of drunkenness appropriate to it, with 0 being a totally booze-free affair like a Halloween Party at your kid's school, and 5 being a party the Greeks would be proud of (see page 148 for inebriation level chart; you will notice a sixth level, but no party should ever go to six, trust me). It is the Drinker's duty to keep the party at its optimum inebriation level. If you notice a party going above it's average—say a birthday party where nearly everyone looks like they are about to take a nap—you can bring the average down by steering into sobriety. On the other hand, if a party needs to be *more* drunk, you know what to do.

Oh and of course, none of this applies if you are in the responsibile role at the party: e.g. you're the designated driver.

SURPRISE PARTY (PRESURPRISE)

INEBRIATION RATING: 1.857

No one wants to mess up the surprise, so your inebriation level should remain low before the guest of honor arrives.

SURPRISE PARTY (POSTSURPRISE)

INEBRIATION RATING: 3.75

After the surprise, however, inebriation levels should shoot through the roof for nearly everyone in attendance. The sense of accomplishment and shared exuberance—*We did it! Were you surprised? You should have seen your face!*—combined with the restraint everyone exercised presurprise calls for a good, drunken evening. If you want to host a party where you can get wasted, this is the one.

BIRTHDAY PARTY (FOR AN ADULT)

INEBRIATION RATING: 3.125

More than any other (besides, perhaps, a bachelor/bachelor-ette party, see page 48), a birthday party focuses on one person and that one person's enjoyment. It is frankly shocking what we will put up with from our birthday men and women. Rather than see this in a negative light, the Drinker knows to take advantage of it, even though taking advantage of it may result in brutally hungover carnage for the birthday boy/girl. The rest of the guests at a birthday party play supporting roles to this carnage, allowing it to happen by supplying drinks, shielding the guest of honor from those who might misunderstand their sloppiness for duress, while also protecting the general populace from their (the guest of honor's, that is) flailing and yelling. Often a wing-person can be assigned to "follow and wallow", matching the same inebriation level as the guest of honor. This is a sacred role, played usually by the same person who would be the best man or maid of honor if this were a wedding (for more on weddings, see page 71).

BIRTHDAY PARTY (FOR A CHILD)

INEBRIATION RATING: 2

At this party, the guest of honor cannot drink but may have the sense and coordination of someone who is *very, very drunk*. As one of the token adults in attendance, you should keep yourself in check, one or two drinks if the parents of the birthday kid are also having one or two.

DINNER PARTY

INEBRIATION RATING: 2.667

A dinner party should be about as tame as it sounds, which explains its inebriation rating coming in at below 3. The intimacy of the occasion, the fact that its main focus is the eating of dinner, and the concept of dinner parties as something that adults do all make this the ideal setting for one cocktail and a couple glasses of wine.

BLOCK PARTY

INEBRIATION RATING: 4

A block party has a high average inebriation rating because of its unique combination of elements: It is outside, often decentralized, generally long, and involves many people, some of whom you are not going to know. This can end up being the perfect storm for drinking a lot and no one really noticing.

GARDEN PARTY

INEBRIATION RATING: 2.5

Garden parties are like gentle outdoor dinner parties that happen in the afternoon. As you are generally not ending your day at a garden party, you can't just open up the drinking throttle. Also, being outside in the sun means that inebriation leads pretty quickly to napping. Also, you are in a garden, which makes everything sleepy and gentle. This is a great opportunity for lower-proof cocktails. I also like gin & tonics over beer here because the sugar in the tonic keeps a pep in your step.

BACKYARD PARTY

INEBRIATION RATING: 3.333

A *backyard* party differs from a garden party in that there is almost 100% more chance of a kiddie pool and some barbecue. This is a party that you commit to for the whole day, so while inebriation levels can be high, they also need pacing. This is where a lager is going to be better than an ale beer-wise, and white wine is gonna be better than red. Similar to the garden party, however, napping is going to be your biggest foe, so pace with water and get up off your chair every once in a while to throw a Frisbee.

WEDDING SHOWER

INEBRIATION RATING: 2.875

Unlike a bachelorette party, a wedding shower (most often actually a bridal shower) celebrates the settling down aspect of marriage, and not the chaos and sex of single life. As such, it is often a more staid affair with overly fancy and/or themed cocktails like mint lime wine spritzers, which pack about as much punch as a weak beer. Most everyone should "drink enough to get chatty, but not enough to get catty." Of course, there are a couple of excessive drinking exceptions, one often portrayed in comedic movies is the disillusioned single friend who drinks enough alcohol to ruin the party by going on a ten-minute rant about marriage, and, let's face it, everybody, the absolutely awful decorations.

BABY SHOWER

A baby shower features the lowest inebriation rating because it's generally held in the morning, and the guest of honor likely won't drink at all. It would be unseemly and generally annoying to be a drunken mess. After the baby shower, however, the hostess(es) may polish off whatever champagne is left and go see a movie or something.

Also, it might be cute if you prepared cocktails ahead of time and then served them in baby bottles.

DANCE PARTY

INEBRIATION RATING: 3.625

While "dance party" can be a catchall term for many different types of parties where dancing occurs, what *all* dance parties share is a need for everyone there to be absolutely wasted. As the saying goes, "On a dance floor, no one can hear your slurred speech." Alcohol aids all attendees of a dance party, whether they enjoy dancing or not. For those who find it embarrassing, alcohol obviously loosens them up and allows them to participate but, equally as important, alcohol also roughs up the moves of those who clearly enjoy dancing *too much*. No one wants a dance floor of crisp choreography. It's intimidating and show-offy. Alcohol equalizes the floor—raising the quality of dancing where needed, lowering it in other places.

It is also worth mentioning that the dance floor is one of the few public places where adult humans get to be overtly sexual, so one often needs the bravery alcohol can provide.

BACHELOR/BACHELORETTE PARTY

INEBRIATION RATING: 3.5

Bachelor and bachelorette parties hold a special place in drinking culture. Like with twenty-first birthdays, fraternity parties, and working in a newsroom, the bachelor or bachelorette can never be too drunk, nor the party too crazy. They often mark the extremes of drunken behavior, with pioneers on a frontier of inebriation as of yet unexplored. It is like a birthday that happens only once (or that's what the guest of honor is thinking), and so every allowance is made for this person to get supremely fucked up. Everyone around the bachelor or bachelorette must aid in this quest, some by also getting supremely fucked up, others by remaining relatively straight ("relatively" being the operative word here) so that they can remind the person about to get married that marriage is probably worth it, and also drive drunken folks home at the end of the night.

COSTUME PARTY

INEBRIATION RATING: 4

You are in costume. They are in costume. EVERYONE IS IN COSTUME. I am not saying no one knows who you are—nor am I recommending you actually try and remain creepily anonymous the entire night—but the night is already weird, and you already don't look exactly like yourself. A lot will be forgiven and forgotten is all I am saying.

HOUSEWARMING PARTY

INEBRIATION RATING: 3

A housewarming is like a really special dinner party (see page 45), with most guests touching the Inebriation Level 3 pole and then quickly leaving and going to their own homes so they can talk about what a weird house that was. And why would anyone live in that neighborhood? The hosts are there to serve, promote, and protect the house. They should remain alert enough to ensure none of their guests spill anything on the rugs, or put a glass down without a coaster.

GRADUATION PARTY

INEBRIATION RATING: 2.5

The graduation party celebrates the hard work, achievement, and good sense it takes to graduate from school. As such, it isn't a good place for Drinkers to actually drink. The guest of honor must play the role of the graduate: shaking hands, accepting congratulations, discussing future plans. It is not a place for the Dionysian chaos of Drinkers. This is a place for those manners you learned so long ago—"yes, sir"s and "yes, ma'am"s all around.

PINK SLIP PARTY

INEBRIATION RATING: 3.75

Similar to the graduation party, the pink slip party also celebrates hard work, achievement, and good sense . . . although with an unhappy ending. Unlike the graduate, the fired person will likely be suffering from no happy vision of the future. And so, where the graduate must step into the new role of a responsible adult, the fired can simply raise his or her glass and say: "I'm done." All the participants at a pink slip party are obliged to join in the celebratory wallowing particular to this type of party.

LAN PARTY

INEBRIATION RATING: 1

If you know what a LAN party is,[5] then you know they aren't alcohol-heavy events. This is because the drug of choice at a LAN party is the hardcore video-game slaughter of your gaming nerd friends. Those who choose to actually drink will be so quickly beaten and are so obviously out of step with the *point of this party* that either their drinking behavior will be modified or they will leave. As such, you will find very few Drinkers at this type of party.

---

5   If you don't, that's because you weren't into computer games as a kid in the 90s. LAN stands for Local Area Network. It's a video game party basically. Don't worry about it.

CAST OR WRAP PARTY

No single party type allows for more downright debauchery than the cast or wrap party, which is thrown following the completion of a theatrical play or a movie. The cast party combines a number of elements, each of which would be more than enough reason on their own to drink oneself to a high rating, but when combined create an inebriation vortex in which reason and restraint lose all power and meaning. These elements are:

1. The feeling of release that comes from the completion of something.

2. The sadness of something ending, *especially* something you shared with people you may not see again soon.

3. The close bonds formed when doing something as time-consuming and silly as putting on a play.

4. Theater and movie people, who are generally drunks and also usually attractive.

5. This is one party where multiple people may have actually had magic and/or clown training. If you find yourself there, go with the flow, but try not to get involved in any spontaneous mime battles.

AFTER-PARTY

If you have made it to an after-party, then two things are usually true: (1) You got invited to the after-party (good for you!), and (2) you are inebriated enough that going to the after-party seems like a good idea. The after-party presents a particular conundrum for all revelers, not least of all to Drinkers: It requires a desire to keep partying at precisely the time when normal human, non-drug-induced energy starts to flag. In order to actually enjoy and capitalize upon the after-party then, you must somehow get your party second wind. Truthfully, alcohol cannot help here. Except in rare cases, alcohol past 1:00 or 2:00 a.m. no longer energizes you. It would be hard for me to count the number of times I took an additional drink because I wanted to keep my own party going, only for that additional drink to be precisely what brought the party to a screeching halt. This conundrum is not specific to the after-party, of course, but the after-party is the perfect distillation of that conundrum: If you stop drinking, the party stops, but if you continue to drink, the party also stops.

To address this, I suggest most everyone actually *stop* drinking at the after-party. The trick to coasting at an inebriation level of 3 is to stop drinking and realize that perfection is fleeting and the attempt to hold on to it will invariably crush it. It is time to go home and hang up your party hat for the night.

FRAT/SORORITY PARTY

What can I say about fraternity parties that has not already been said? The whole system is set up for maximum drunkenness. I cannot stand in its way and so offer this guide simply as a reflection of reality. My one suggestion, for those frat brothers and sorority sisters intelligent and inquisitive enough to be reading this manual, is to maybe go against the grain. Think of it as practice for the adult parties you'll throw later in life. Set up *your* frat/sorority party as a cocktail enthusiast's option in contrast to the beer-and-vodka-soaked versions provided elsewhere. Serve confusing and complicated classics like the Vieux Carré; require that people dress nicely and wait for their drinks; hire an old-timey jazz vocalist.

If you must, you *may* serve your Vieux Carrés out of a plastic garbage can.

OTHER VARIABLES THAT WILL
AFFECT YOUR PARTY DRINKING

Adjustments and exceptions to party inebriation ratings can be made in certain cases, depending on the state of the Drinker at a particular party. If any of the following apply to you, you should adjust the inebriation rating, as needed. Please note you cannot go above a 6 or below a 0, and so these adjusted ratings are confined within those limits. It was once believed that there were inebriation ratings above 6. For reasons the author *would rather not get into*, those levels have been disproven.

PARTY VARIABLES	INEBRIATION RATING ADJUSTMENTS
You'd rather not be there.	-1
You do not like the host and/or guest of honor.	-2
You are single.	+1
The party sucks.	+2
You are overdressed.	+1
You are underdressed.	+2
Your date has ditched you.	+1
You have ditched your date.	+2
A famous person is at the party.	-1
That famous person is Keifer Sutherland.	+3
You have to work in the morning.	-1
You live in New York City.	+1
There are fatty snacks like nachos served at the party.	+1
You are a politician or say things like, "I can't. I might run for office one day."	-3
You went to the gym that day.	+1
The more you drink, the sadder you feel.	-2
The more you drink, the better you feel.	+1

Valentine's Day

There's no way to discuss Valentine's Day without choosing sides. It is less a holiday than a very specific ritual involving roses, satin, candlelight, chocolate, and champagne. Combine them just so, we are told, and you alchemically create romance. You either enjoy the ritual and all the silky fabric that goes with it, or you don't.

While I will stay out of the pro/con debate over Valentine's Day, I will always choose a side when it comes to drinking. On February 14, I ask you to join me in saying: Screw all those stupid Valentine's Day drinks. No self-respecting adult should drink anything called a "love potion," and there is something vaguely threatening about anyone who uses the word "aphrodisiac." Your Valentine's Day drinks menu should reflect you and your actual role within this yearly ritual. Not all of us are in a satin-and-bubble-bath relationship. Some of us will be spending the holiday alone; others couldn't care less; others will still do their damndest to actually ruin other people's evenings. Whoever you are this V-Day, choose your drink wisely and accordingly.

Drinks from Least Romantic
to Most Romantic

LEAST ROMANTIC

Any drink that takes two hands to hold

Any drink that comes with a side of buffalo wings

Any drink you "shoot" (unless maybe, OK, you are shooting it off another person's body, but that's more sexy than romantic, yeah?)

High balls. Low on the list mostly because the drink involves the words "high" and "balls"

Bottled drinks

Drinks that come from a tap or are served in anything resembling a stein

Drinks garnished with an olive

Drinks with so-called aphrodisiac ingredients—it might "sound" romantic, but like I said above, there is something just not right here

White wine

Drinks with a sugared rim

Manly looking drinks served in rocks glasses

Pink wine

Red wine

Anything with bubbles. Sparkling wine is a like a diamond in this way—we have been conditioned to connect them with romance

MOST ROMANTIC

THE COUPLE THAT JUST GOT
TOGETHER TWO WEEKS AGO

This is my favorite couple to observe out on Valentine's Day—the people who just started dating, like, two weeks ago. Don't they know better? In fact, there should be a whole reality show about these types. "Melinda likes George, but are these two ready to eat by candlelight?" V-Day is an all-or-nothing proposition. Alas, romance doesn't come in a "lite" version—and these poor people always bear that weight awkwardly.

If you find yourself in an early relationship and forced to go out on V-Day, avoid drinking anything remotely big-R Romantic. I mean, don't be a weirdo about it—don't go out and order a yard-stick of beer, or something. Stick to something innocuous and classy. Perfect drink here: a sidecar. Festive, but without any of the heavy symbolism that could lead to a panic attack.

THE RECENTLY BROKEN-UP

Depends. Are you sad or angry? Were you the dumpee or the dumper? You know what? Doesn't matter.

Drive to your nearest college town and order the shots most likely to make you blush when saying their names out loud. This is a night when you can justifiably say, "Another Wyoming Legspreader" and no one will mess with you. Just say, "You know what, I just broke up with my boy- (or girl-) friend," and everyone will back off.

LONG-TERM COUPLES WHO
SERIOUSLY COULDN'T CARE LESS

I will hazard a guess that a lot of couples would put themselves in this category on February 14. Sure, you like the other person, but you don't need to spend $75 a head on some limp surf and turf to prove it. Rather than pressure yourselves to live up to some passion you left behind at around year three, I recommend you skip it. Unlike all those people out at dinner saying stuff like "Omigosh, I also love Tahoe!" or whatever, you get to enjoy the benefits of a long-term relationship. Which are these: Get into your pajamas, rent a movie starring that Tim Riggins guy, and give a little tip of the hat to V-Day by opening a bottle of red wine. Each.

LONG-TERM COUPLES TRYING
TO RECAPTURE EARLY PASSION

Of course, not all long-term relationships have the luxury of not caring about lost passion. We all go through those phases when it seems important to rekindle some early relationship energy. If you're going through one, then you may actually need to follow the V-Day script, at least a little bit. In the absence of spontaneous romance, you may want to surround you and your S.O. with the usual symbols of romance.

So, fine: get some champagne, if you must, but be careful—champage can carry a lot of capital-R Romantic pressure. I recommend a rosé here. It will feel romantic and special—it's pink!—but with a casualness that can take the pressure off.

V-DAY HATERS

For some, Valentine's Day is an invitation to hate Valentine's Day. Defining yourself by your enemies doesn't seem like the best strategy for a fun evening, but someone has to wage war against the greeting card companies, I suppose.

Your drink? Pour a bottle of champagne down the drain while nursing a forty.

YOUR PARTNER REALLY LOVES VALENTINE'S DAY

While there are many ways to screw up Valentine's Day, the stakes are never higher than if you are with someone who genuinely loves the holiday.

Get two crystal flutes, fill halfway with assorted berries, top with champagne, and garnish with an entire bouquet of roses. I don't know how you're going to fit the whole bouquet in there, but you are set up to fail here anyway, so you may as well go down swinging.

The Winter Holidays

While Christmas and Hanukkah aren't drinking holidays per se, they are the holiday that presents the most reasons to drink: family time, shopping crowds, end-of-year ennui, sweater-laden parties, holiday music; the list goes on. It is no wonder that most people run the holiday gauntlet with a drink in hand.

DRINKING TO DEAL WITH YOUR FAMILY

When you are under eighteen, or so, the holidays mean presents and wearing your dress pants; when you are over eighteen, the focus shifts away from presents to way-less-fun-to-unwrap family dynamics.

If you are visiting them

Visiting family for the holidays involves the trifecta of seasonal stress: travel, sleeping in someone else's house, and, of course, your relatives. To top it off, your relatives usually have shitty booze. The last time I tried mixing a drink at my parents' house, I was forced to work with a dusty bottle of Smirnoff, a sticky bottle of Rose's lime juice, and an unopened bottle of Baileys. THAT WAS IT. Why did my parents have an unopened bottle of Baileys?

So my suggestion: Bring your own bar and anoint yourself the bartender. TAKE OVER, is what I am saying. So much of the holiday travel scenario is out of your control—delayed flights, forced interaction with your uncle's girlfriend, the unholy volume at which your mom plays John Denver's Christmas album, so you need to build a liquor kingdom and declare yourself ruler.

Most of your relatives will be thrilled to become subjects in your kingdom. It's not that they want to only drink wine, it's that they do not know how to drink. Simply slicing a fresh lemon peel for a martini will blow their minds. "So fancy!" most of them will say.

If they are visiting you

Almost the opposite goes if you are *hosting* your family. In that case, you have too much control, and your house is full of people messing with your stuff. People are coming to you with questions all the time—"Uncle Matthew, where is the glue?"—and your parents are passive-aggressively commenting on your cooking skills: "Oh, that's an interesting way to do it."

So basically, drink all day. Get loose! Let your stuff get messed with! The kitchen cabinets get glued shut by your niece? Hilarious! Your parents tell you a very long story about shopping for socks, and you'll never guess who they ran into? Tell me more! Have a tumbler of whiskey with you at all times. Don't pound beers or drink from a wine glass—that looks too much like drinking, and carrying around a wine glass is just not practical. Get a nice solid tumbler that can be put down easily on fireplace mantels, coffee tables, and carpets where puzzles are being put together.

In order not to get totally jollied up, add ice to the whiskey.

A special note on eggnog

While very heavily associated with Christmas, eggnog is also crazy rich—eggs! sugar! milk! heavy cream! rum!—so reserve its consumption for the more extreme moments of Christmas celebration, such as, oh I don't know, bringing a dead tree into your house and decorating it with tiny lights and dangly things you made when you were in the second grade.

OFFICE HOLIDAY PARTY

What makes the office holiday party so simultaneously wonderful and awful is how often it turns into a shit show. In this way, it resembles a high school prom—take a bunch of people with different statuses whose normal interactions are completely different than those we normally associate with a party; and then ill-advisedly pour a bunch of alcohol into them.

To paraphrase Chekov, if you introduce an open bar at the beginning of the office party, then someone from sales must—and will—don his tie like a bandanna by the end of the party. This is the catch-22 of the office holiday party. Adding alcohol can reduce the awkwardness of combining work relationships with holiday merriment, but it almost always leads to things way more awkward when seen in the harsh light of sobriety. Going duet with your boss on a karaoke version of "It's Raining Men" will not be something either you or she will wish to remember the following Monday.

So what are we office workers to do? Avoid the tipple all night and stick to gritting our teeth? I don't think that is necessary. Not all offices are alike, of course, and getting a little loose may be totally appropriate. The question is how loose. Just like high school, holiday office parties locate themselves right on the boundary of personal embarrassment; to succeed amidst its environs, you need to know how far over that line you are able to go and still retain your dignity.

What kind of company do you work for?

In terms of your opponent (i.e., the company who pays your healthcare) you must consider whether it is a cool company or a serious company. On the surface this may seem simple to discern—"serious" companies require business attire; while "cool" companies look like a television version of a college dorm room (posters! cereal! people on skateboards!).

While that is an OK place to start, you don't want to make your entire office holiday party drinking decisions based on whether your workplace is cool with you wearing shorts and Adidas sandals to a meeting. In the holiday party sense, you need to know how the company (and coworkers) will react when you become the party version of yourself. The closer your work identity already is to your party identity, the cooler the company.

So in order to asses how many drinks you can knock back at the party, you must first discern: what kind of company do you work for? If you need help, consult this checklist on the next page.

COOL COMPANY CHECKLIST:

___ Employee count is under twenty-five OR
median employee age is under twenty-five.

___ You have been hungover at work *and acknowledged
it* at least once in the past week.

___ Your company name has the word "Urban"
and/or "Outfitters" in it.

___ The office fridge always has beer in it.

___ Your music tastes are known to others and
actually matter to them.

___ When you ask your boss about the weekend, he or
she starts with, "Well, have you ever taken mushrooms?"

___ The name of your company has no vowels in it.

SERIOUS COMPANY CHECKLIST:

___ When you were hired, it was assumed you would
be joining a golf club.

___ The majority of your day is spent in meetings.

___ You issue press releases regularly.

___ Nobody around you sports a beard or any facial
hair whatsoever.

___ Your boss was caught in a highly publicized sex
and/or drug scandal.

What do you do at the office?

Once you have established the context of your party—i.e., whether your company is cool or serious—then you must take a long look at yourself. Basically you need to answer: How much embarrassment can I *really* get away with?

This depends less on your personal charm and more on your role within the company—and whether anyone at your office would really actually mess with you if you did get a little sauced. Would anyone fire Han Solo, for instance, if he were drunk at a holiday office party? No. Of course they wouldn't. They put up with Solo—drunk, misogynist, whatever—because he can make the f'ing Kessel Run in less than twelve parsecs, goddammit. Boss or not, you can get away with a lot if you are Han f'ing Solo.

Most of us are not Han Solo, of course, and so we must look to our actual positions to understand the amount of alcohol appropriate when partying with our coworkers. Consult the list of job roles below before your next office holiday party.

INTERN

Cool—1 drink

How old are you, anyway? I'm sure you had to work really hard to get this internship at Warp Records, or whatever, but please: just stick with the weed we all know you have on you. No drinks for you.

Unless . . . could we get a little of that weed? OK: one glass of wine.

Serious—0 drinks

You also get no drinks, but you probably don't even want them, do you? You want to be sharp as a tack so if that senior partner comes striding by, you can impress him or her with your analysis of the current market conditions of your industry. Good for you, but guess what? That senior partner is wasted.

ENTRY-LEVEL

Cool—1 drink

Oh wow, you just graduated with a marketing degree! You are basically an intern without the weed, so see above.

Serious—0 drinks

Ibid.

PERIPHERAL

You work in the kitchen, clean the place, keep the servers running—i.e., no one knows your name, but without you the whole place would collapse in seconds.

Cool—4 drinks

No one knows your name, right? Flying under the radar has its benefits, including getting this superhip company to pay for your drinks all night. The trick to this one is staying under the radar, however. You probably don't want to sling back four Long Island iced teas. Start with cocktails and move to beer.

Serious—2 drinks

Sorry, you get fewer drinks than your cool-company counterpart, simply because the radar you fly under is a lot more perceptive. This is a company where you don't want them to know your name. Stay off the grid, and you'll be safe. Beer is best here—but hopefully they are springing for the expensive stuff.

PLATEAUED COG IN THE MACHINE

Cool—5 drinks

If you self-identify as a plateaued cog in the machine—i.e., you have come to terms with the fact that being an advertising copywriter is just like any other desk job, even if you are "working in publishing"; and also you don't care about moving up the ladder because it sucks just as bad up there—if this is you, it's time to drown your sorrows. Five drinks, all spirits, stick to twist garnishes.

Serious—5 drinks

You have the job they make fun of in movies and TV shows like *Office Space* and *The Office* and are in much need of sorrow-drowning. Five drinks and the only difference from cool company is that you will take olives or other such salty garnish.

MIDDLE MANAGEMENT

Cool—3 drinks

People report to you; you report to people—that is your whole job. But when you work at a cool company, it is important that you buck the "middle management" stereotype; your company culture depends on it. You can get a little loose, but be careful not to cross the line. Two cocktails, max (but something cool like an old-fashioned, if possible), then a glass of wine.

Serious—1 drinks

Most people at your office are managers, so no stereotype to defy. You want to move up to senior management (where they can't drink at all as you'll see, so watch out), so stay clearheaded and focused. A glass of wine or beer–no spirits for you.

SKILLED LABOR

Cool—3 drinks

You have some special skill the suits can't easily replace. Either you actually studied science or computers; or you have convinced your liberal arts boss that "content strategy" or "community manager" is actually a job. Either way, have fun tonight–you are the eccentric talent that the company is built around!–but remember: there are more people than you think who can write computer code, so don't lose your head. Three drinks–all cocktails–each one different.

Serious—4 drinks

Same as above, except your skills make even more money for your company. Add one more cocktail.

SENIOR MANAGEMENT

Cool—1 drinks

Good for you. You are shepherding this cool company through the realities of actually making money. In your head, you dream of public offerings and acquisitions. You were the one who brought in the sales team; who introduced the whole idea of quarterly goals; who questioned whether the office really needed a video game room. In a word, you are responsible, and your whole business plan depends on it. One drink—glass of wine or beer ONLY—just to show the kids that you are not totally square.

Serious—0 drinks

Someone's got to keep an eye on the boss (see below).

THE BOSS

Cool—2 drinks

When you started this company in your garage, you had no idea it would grow to even have a holiday party! This should be a time to celebrate, but hold on. Just because you are cool does not mean you get to act like a jackass and hit on the intern. You are the public face of a cool company, sure, but it's not the friggin' Stones. Have two cocktails by all means, but stop there.

Serious—5+ drinks

You are the 1 percent, so you can do whatever you want and no one can touch you. You probably have people employed just to cover up the dumb shit you get yourself into (see Senior Management). Enjoy the spoils, king or queen.

Exceptions to the above

There are a few on-the-ground considerations that can adjust your office holiday party drink total. Please review this chart and adjust accordingly.

EXCEPTIONS	DRINK ADJUSTMENTS
Your immediate boss is drunk.	+1
There is only snack food.	-2
There is an open bar and a sit-down dinner.	+1
There is an open bar but no food.	Get the hell out of there *right now*.
You secretly love someone at your office, and either they or you are married.	-5 (or whatever takes you down to 0)
You secretly love someone at your office, and both of you are single.	+2 (and check your teeth)
Wrestling of any type is occurring (mud, jello, arm)	+3
There are circus and/or zoo animals.	+1 for each species
Your hear the phrase, "I'd like to introduce you to one of our investors."	-1 for each time you hear that phrase

Weddings

There aren't many scenarios in your life when you will encounter a true open bar—your office holiday party maybe, some art and culture events if you run in those circles, a party at Kanye West's house—which is what makes weddings so damn awesome. Not only are open bars the norm for weddings, but cash bars are actually *looked down upon* and tend to cause complaining (at least in the online wedding forums where I hang out). An open bar has its downsides, of course. Like college kids at their first frat party, people can be driven a little crazy by the sheer and profound access to booze, which is why we end up with train-wreck best man speeches and uncles doing that weird crouching/jumping Russian dance.

Weddings are organized like Mafia families—it is no mistake that *The Godfather* opens with a f'ing wedding—with concentric circles of lessening importance around the bride and groom (and Marlon Brando). The farther out you are, the less influence you have on the outcome, and thus the more potentially drunk and selfish you can be. It's not big news when your cousin hits on your friend from fourth grade; but when the maid of honor does it, it won't escape notice.

Of course, you never want to cross the line from drunk to special-day-ruiner. *Anyone* can fuck up a wedding by punching someone out on the dance floor or trying to sleep with the groom.

Every wedding has essentially the same structure, no matter how many anarchist stickers the bride and/or groom have on their laptop:

- Rehearsal dinner the night before
- Getting-ready rituals for the wedding party
- Ceremony/vows
- Reception

This schedule is your playing field. Here's how to play it, based on your role.

WEDDING PARTY

Since folks in the wedding party participate in every wedding event—including perhaps a bachelor or bachelorette party—the strategy here is pacing, hydration, and grabbing rest when you can. Unlike other wedding jobs, being a member of the WP means you are central to the celebration. You must both have fun *and be highly visible during fun*—dicey territory, if ever there were any.

Overall strategy: Stick to drinks that convey celebration, and avoid drinking when unnecessary (like after the rehearsal dinner back at your hotel or whatever).

Rehearsal dinner: Two or three glasses of champagne—enough to give you confidence and be social, but not enough to make shots at the local dive bar seem like a good idea.

Getting-ready rituals: One glass of champagne *if the bride or groom offers a toast*. Otherwise, leave your flask at home and drink coffee, water, and power-chew some good-old B12.

Ceremony/vows: Should be obvious, but don't try and sneak anything while standing beside the bride and groom. I have heard stories of groomsmen taking swigs before they escort someone down the aisle. Bad idea. Remember, you are visible (and likely being recorded) and wearing nice clothes.

Reception: Home stretch! You can open up the throttle a little here: People *expect* shoeless bridesmaids and headband-tie-wearing groomsmen on the dance floor. I find gin and tonics to be a good wedding drink—slightly hydrating, and the sugar in the tonic will give you the energy you need to represent during "Bust a Move." Have one glass of wine with dinner and then switch to G&Ts. Pace it about one an hour. And do I need to say it? Match each drink with a glass of water or two. Again, do whatever it takes to avoid shots. Please.

COLLEGE FRIEND

You know how they say that you tend to regress back to the person you were when you hang out with people from your past? Lucky you, college friend! For one night you get to relive those glory years before hangovers. For college friends, weddings serve as auxiliary ten-year reunions; and in all likelihood, you don't really know the family all that well. As such, you can fly under the radar a bit. As long as you don't get in the way of the wedding, there's no reason it should obstruct your goals of seeing your friends and meeting a hot cousin.

Rehearsal dinner: If you are invited, you actually have the responsibility of meeting the family and getting involved. Drink two glasses of wine and meet everyone at the bar later. Keep your drinking mellow and conversation focused: two cocktails or three beers paced over a couple hours.

Preceremony: Fill your flask with some better-than-college-quality whiskey and start sipping.

Ceremony: Don't drink while at the ceremony—there's too much risk you'll get caught and, really, that type of behavior probably indicates that you should check in to Betty Ford after the wedding.

Reception: Line up shots of tequila with your friends at the bar, toast to their health and your friendship, and shoot 'em back. Do another in honor of the bride and groom, and then switch to beer and whatever is left in your flask. Ask the bride's mother or father to dance, and you will go down in family history in a good way.

EXTENDED FAMILY

Oddly, the familial roles are switched at weddings: The younger generation wants to show everyone that they are no longer the awkward kids everyone remembers from weddings past; the older generation, on the other hand, wants to show the kids that they don't have a monopoly on fun. The basic strategies: If you are under forty, you drink less; if you are over forty, you get to drink more.

Rehearsal dinner: If you are a younger member of the extended family, come out strong here with your "I'm an adult" move. If cocktails are available, go for a gin martini straight up with a twist. Don't order anything with a straw, for god's sake. But stick to that and one glass of wine—you don't want to overplay your hand. If you are in the older generation, stick to two glasses of wine or beer—you aren't as young as you used to be, and you need all the energy you have for that Russian crouch dance you love bringing out.

Preceremony and ceremony: Nothing—you are gonna have to kiss grandma's cheek, and you don't want to be smelling like bourbon. And grandma—people are gonna be kissing your cheek, so you don't want to be smelling like bourbon eith—. . . Actually, scratch that. Grandma gets at least two fingers of Scotch before the ceremony.

Reception: Seeing your family members on the dance floor is one of the great joys and necessary horrors of life. The drinking strategy for extended family ensures that it happens. Younger generation: Shadow the wedding party and drink gin and tonics with them—THROW OUT THE STRAW, and keep your eye out for college friends trying to hit on you. Older generation: Do shots with the college friends, and then switch to white wine and water. If you are the Marlon Brando of your family and need to hold court somewhere quiet, then you drink super-expensive Scotch, obviously.

Class Reunions, Organized by Year

REUNION YEAR	GOAL	HOW DRINKING CAN HELP
5	Showing people how different you are from five years ago.	Drink cocktails. Cocktails definitely show people how sophisticated you are.
10	Showing people how successful you are. Also: sex.	Buy drinks for everyone as long as you can swing it. Buying drinks for people at this age blows people away because they spend most of their lives trying to avoid paying for drinks.
20	Showing people how similar you are to twenty years ago. Sex, too.	Alcohol lowers inhibitions and makes it possible to talk to that woman, Misty, you had a crush on when you were sixteen.
30	Sharing with people how unhappy you really are and how your kids are mostly disappointing and you are fatter than you want to be.	Make a lot of toasts. Drinking makes communal sorrow special and ritualistic.
40	Accepting how fat you are and how old everyone is and so who cares, have fun, dance.	Drink so that you don't feel your age on the dance floor.
50	Discussions about grandkids. Sex.	To be honest, drink may not add anything when you hit this milestone, but I can guarantee this: it also won't take anything away!

Gambling

Gambling presents Drinkers with one of their very few *defensive* drinking situations. Casinos and other gambling establishments (such as airports in Nevada and alleyways in old Broadway musicals) use alcohol against you so that you will lose more money. They take all the standard benefits of liquor—it emboldens you, reduces your pain, adds a flourish to your dice throwing—and flip them so that they become your weaknesses. Being emboldened, flamboyant, and impervious to loss and embarrassment makes you great on the dance floor, but horrible at gambling.

The casinos know this, of course, and so quite literally give alcohol away. The first time I entered a House of Chance, I couldn't believe my luck. "You mean all I must do is sit at this table and play cards, and an attractive woman wearing a show-girl outfit will simply bring me drinks?" It seemed too good to be true. By the end of the night, my heroically large bar tab—even I was surprised how many Manhattans I had drunk—came to $0.00; but if you included my gambling tab, then my seven Manhattans cost me about $200 each. I learned the hard way: Casinos are even better at drinking than I am.

Is a Drinker simply not to consume alcohol at all within a casino, then? Certainly that is an option. But just as gamblers believe they can beat the house at their game of chance, I believe there are ways to beat them at their game of drinking.

While I cannot promise that you will win money, I can assure you that no one at the gambling establishment will mistake you for an amateur Drinker.

The goal while drinking in a casino or other gambling establishment is to drink as *much* as you can while gambling as *little* as you can. In gambling circles, this is called "comp hustling"; in drinking circles, we just call it "good sense." Most casinos give away alcohol as part of their comp system, i.e., free stuff they give to patrons to reward them for gambling. The more you gamble, and the more money you wager, the more comps the casino will issue you. Alcohol is considered the first level of comp, available pretty much to anyone who is gambling. This works to the advantage of Drinkers, as unlike other comp hustlers, their reward comes at a much lower cost than, say, a free hotel room or the really high-roller stuff, like the opportunity to take a bath with a panther, or whatever other outlandish things only rich people dream up.

The trick is to make it look like you are gambling, or that you would be gambling *a lot* if you only had one more drink. On the following page, you'll find a few of the strategies Drinkers have used for generations in order to drink the house under the table.

- Make a big show of only gambling when you are good and liquored up. Accept drinks on the house, and then leave before actually wagering anything.

- Hang out with old ladies playing slot machines and add your drink order to theirs when the cocktail waitress swings by.

- Impersonate and dress like a high roller and accept all their comps. Like a real actual high roller. Just be prepared to run if the actual person you are impersonating walks through the doors.

- Play poker, the gambling game in which you never have to gamble beyond the ante or blinds and so can sit there for quite a while just sucking down drinks and enjoying the action at the table.

Other Defensive Drinking Scenarios

Gambling is not the only scenario in which Drinkers must fend themselves from weaponized drink. Here are some more situations in which alcohol might be being used against you:

- Being a woman in a public place
- Cocktail parties full of spies
- Ukranian nightclubs during the day (Trust me. Long story.)
- Games of Scrabble played with very competitive people
- Psychotherapy sessions
- Anything called a "drinking game"
- Anything called an "alcohol war"
- Business dinners

Movies [6]

Drinking is a wonderful accompaniment to enjoying the cinema. Sadly, most American movie theaters and palaces forbid alcohol and don't offer anything stronger than Lemonheads. While you can attempt to recreate the theater experience at home, where the drinking laws are more relaxed, there is nothing quite like drinking with a silent crowd all staring the same direction. In this, drinking at the movies resembles sitting at a very large, very dark dive bar.

There are movie theaters that serve alcohol, but they are few and far between. Most of your major cities (and many of the more important weed-friendly towns: Austin, Madison, Asheville) will have them.

But should you not have access to one of these establishments, or you don't want to see the horror/camp classic or whichever Richard Linklater movie they happen to be playing, then you will have to provide the liquor yourself. This presents challenges, but also, for the prepared Drinker, some wonderful opportunities!

6 See also Sneaking It Where It's Illegal, page 101.

YOU SUCK AT DRINKING

THE FOUR SIMPLE, NEVER-FAIL STEPS FOR GETTING LIQUOR INTO A MOVIE THEATER

- Decide your vessel.

- Decide your drink.

- Devise and build an elaborate smuggling mechanism, preferably using a large coat with a smaller person hiding inside.

- Smuggle.

Your vessel choices range from the innocent-looking water bottle to the completely-obvious-but-easier-to-slip-into-a-pocket flask. I have seen young Drinkers attempt to sneak liquor in via a jumbo-size soda cup, one much like those they sell in the movie theater itself, and while it can be successful, the gambit also requires that you sneak that jumbo cup past the ticket taker, something no adult wants to be caught doing. Also, then you are drinking alcohol from a big soda cup, which is also something no adult wants to be caught doing.

Once in the theater with your refreshment, wait until at least the previews before taking a sip. Pacing is one of the most challenging aspects of theater drinking. Because movie snacks are meant to be administered with an IV-drip-like steadiness, Drinkers shouldn't act like they are drinking from a pint or rocks glass. This would lead to a drunken surge beneficial for social situations, but totally ineffective for movie watching. Smaller sips over a longer period will create the mild-focused buzz most appropriate for enjoying ninety-plus minutes of story. Go any quicker, and you run the risk of crossing the line into thinking it's appropriate to share your opinions on the plot or special effects with your fellow moviegoers at high volume (for "sudden onset of loud voice" and other bodily sensations a drinker should acquaint themselves with, see page 150).

This will ensure that your alcohol lasts the entire film *and* that you actually remember important plot details, like who the hero was and what that whole scene at the end actually meant, stuff which will come in handy during the rousing discussion likely to take place over postflick drinks.

Because of this pace (and the limitations of your vessel), many drinks are not recommended. Beer would look ridiculous in a water bottle and would be unpleasantly warm by about a third of the way through the film. Tiki drinks may taste like the Snapple sold at the concession stand, but the umbrellas and pineapple garnish make it too conspicuous for any but the most elaborate smugglers.

Instead, Drinkers should consider straight whiskey, or, my personal favorite, gin and tonic in the water bottle. It looks like fizzy water, and the sugar in the tonic keeps me sharp enough to follow the twists and turns of even the most complicated action movies.

Television

Television is a "guilty pleasure," as they say. To remove that stain of guilt, apply an appropriate serving of alcohol and scrub.

As one would expect, the art of drinking *with* television depends greatly on what one is watching *on* television. The equation is thus: The greater the guilt, the greater amount of booze required. This does not mean one should aim for oblivion—you are trying to enjoy a television program, not a wedding. Instead, you should arrange to drink steadily and consistently for as long as you sit in front of the tube. This means choosing a liquor with a proof appropriate to your drinking level. This might be wine or it might be absinthe, it doesn't matter. All that matters is that you enjoy your programs guilt-free.

Cocktails are not advised, as they require getting up from your couch to make them. If you'd like hard liquor, but do not wish to drink straight spirits, any of your highballs would be a wonderful choice—Moscow mule, gin and tonic, even a rum and Coke. Wine might be the ideal television beverage for most; it has a relatively low alcohol content, and you can top your glass off without a return to the fridge.

Certain television events require certain beverages, of course: The Super Bowl only works with beer; the Academy Awards are unwatchable without champagne. But for the most part, you can choose your drink based on the amount of shame and guilt you feel for watching a particular bit of television. For instance: the *PBS NewsHour* is a worthy pursuit and needs no more than a bracing glass of milk. A four-hour marathon of *Storage Wars*, however, calls for some serious intoxification. Turn the page for a list of shows and genres—from least to most guilt-inducing.

SHOWS (FROM LEAST GUILT-INDUCING TO MOST)	DRINK SUGGESTED (BASED ON AVERAGE DRINKER LEVEL)
PBS news	Milk, or perhaps a small glass of vermouth
Network news	White wine with a dash of bitters
Cable news	White wine with a dash of gin
Satirical news	Red wine
Sports	Beer
Any prime-time drama consumed in a normal, human-size stretch of one hour	A cocktail of your choice, you rational adult, you!
Reality programs about animals	Gin and tonic
Game shows (prime time)	7 and 7
Reality programs about animal owners	Gin and tonic and more gin
Reality programs in which people make things and then are judged to death	Champagne cocktail
Reality talent competitions	Whiskey with ice
Awards shows	Champagne
Reality shows with "Fear" in the title	Rum and Coke!
Reality shows about "love"	Straight Chartreuse (with berries)
Game shows (daytime)	Vodka, soda, valium
Sitcoms	What are you doing with your life?
Reruns of sitcoms from when you were a teenager	Zima, or something else you would have drunk when you were fifteen
Any TV consumed in a horror-show unstoppable binge of televisual gluttony	Red wine from a box big enough to last through the marathon TV binge

Unlike drinking for leisure, Drinkers add alcohol to work in order to lessen the pain or boredom of that work, or to lower their resistance to working. It is the same principle that allows you to approach a stranger in a bar or tell your friend how you really feel about his or her dumb haircut. Inhibitions are the roadblocks that your mind puts between you and your true intentions. By removing them, you make all sorts of things possible, including uninteresting things like doing your taxes or mowing the lawn.[7]

As with most things drinking-related, of course, you want to attain the right balance between inebriated courage and sober lucidity. The more mindless a task is, the more alcohol can be mixed with it. So, each type of work should be considered on a scale of acceptable sloppiness in order to find the right type and amount of alcohol to pair with it.

Drinking at the Office

Adding liquor to office work can be complicated, mostly because office work is something from which you can be fired. Because most people work in offices for pay, this can seriously affect their ability to buy liquor. Thus, firing must be avoided at all costs.

---

7   Of course, it's a balance. Having a martini while plowing through your 1040 is one thing; drinking until you see double and can't do simple math will probably lead to some serious hurting come April 15. Same principle goes for lawn-mowing, of course, and most other types of work.

Instead of secretly adding alcohol to your office job to make it bearable, then, I suggest Drinkers employ the sauce in order to do their work better, perhaps even leading to a raise! Below is an analysis of common corporate departments and how alcohol might improve the work done within them.

HUMAN RESOURCES

Human Resources is probably the least-hospitable department when it comes to drinking. The HR department is like the hall monitor of any office. They enforce rules no one really knows and must set an example of behavior no one else follows. And yet, in a brutal catch-22, *because of this* the HR department probably deserves a drink more than any other in the corporate world.

What is an HR manager to do? You might be tempted to sneak your alcohol—vodka in a water bottle, perhaps—but this is not advised for obvious reasons. Should you be outed, your whole system of rules would collapse.

Instead, as the head of official corporate culture, you have the power to institute sanctioned drinking times. Hold a happy hour in your office every day at 4:30, for instance. Not only would you get to use the company card for your liquor, but it would also get other employees on your side, which will be helpful later, when you have to force them to take sexual harassment training.

Suggested Department Drinks: Gin and tonic, rosé, something light and refreshing. Get a SodaStream.

SALES

Culturally, sales has a reputation for heavy drinking, so you start with a net alcohol advantage. But as in the tortoise and the hare, this god-given advantage could also lead to your downfall, which—also like the hare—may come in the form of naps and weirdly timed dessert eating.

In order to keep alcohol on your side in this fight, follow the old sales rule:

One for me, two for the client. Slow and steady wins this race, too.

As long as you are *relatively* sober, you will remain in everyone's good graces.

Suggested Department Drinks: You can expense them, so don't go for cheap beer or well liquor unless it is specifically asked for by the client. Also: No salesperson ever looked bad holding a gin martini.

FINANCE

How much can you drink and still do math? Drink that much.

Suggested Department Drinks: Something big and fruit-filled and umbrella-adorned to counteract the image of you not being any fun. You are totally fun.

CREATIVE

As long as you are generating enough "ideas," a bottle of booze on your desk won't bother anybody. For you, booze should be deployed to strike the fire of inspiration. Studies on alcohol and creativity do exist; if you're feeling the heat from HR for such public displays of drinking, just drop a few links to articles on the science behind booze and creativity on the company intranet or in conversation with somebody from marketing.

Suggested Department Drinks: Bottle of whiskey or vodka, clearly in sight, and drunk straight, with or without ice.

MAINTENANCE/FACILITIES

Oh, the shit that the rest of the company has *no idea about*, am I right? How quickly you could bring things down with the flip of a few switches, the changing of a few locks. While you probably should not use your knowledge and power for destruction, you can leverage it to hide booze basically anywhere you want. Yours is a hiding-in-plain-sight scenario; no one knows the physical layout of the space quite like you, and (I can guarantee you) no one has any idea what you do all day. You are the tortoise here (see Sales, page 87) and can drink small amounts all day, if you want. And then go join the HR department for their 4:30 cocktail hour.

Suggested Department Drinks: Whatever you wish. I encourage strange and lavish drinks, just because you can. Put a blender somewhere. Have a minifridge just for fresh syrups and juices. Install a keg in that that closet only you (and maybe one person in HR) have keys to.

I.T.

Use alcohol to combat your image of being unfriendly and condescending tech nerds. Whether or not they are accurate, movies and television often depict you as a person unwilling to explain or help people whom you think are dumb because they aren't as good as you are with computers. First off, stop acting that way, even though they are, indeed, dumb. And second, create a positive reputation by showing up to help people with beer in tow. You will very quickly become the most popular department in the office, though you might notice that people's computers "break" more often.

Suggested Department Drinks: Beer is good. It can be easily carried and requires no glassware for drinking.

MARKETING

Not quite sales, not quite creative or product development—you sit in between many departments translating and mixing many different elements, which you then serve up to the public. You are the communicator, listening and repeating words more eloquently than the person who originally said them.

Sound like another job you know? That's right: bartenders. Every good marketing employee should be able to mix up drinks right at their desk, whether for spontaneous meetings between stakeholders or for aiding in listening to someone from creative bitching about how their gorgeous print ad is being compromised.

Suggested Department Drinks: Stay simple and agile. No one wants to wait while you sugar the rim for a sidecar. Try Highballs, Negronis, anything you can make without really measuring.

CEO OR OTHER HIGH-LEVEL EXECUTIVE

For many of you in positions of power, a well-timed drink has the ability to soften your image, while an ill-timed one (or two or three or four) has the ability to undermine it. People don't necessarily want a drunk in charge of their employment, but I do believe they want someone who knows how to *handle* a drink. While a teetotaler boss definitely exudes an air of discipline and order, being a true leader requires the ability to keep control during chaos. A seasoned Drinker does this naturally, having honed and trained the voice of reason that only emerges when you are drunk.

And so it is recommended that you head honchos both drink and show yourself in control of your drink. Participate in company-wide parties and cocktail hours, but unless you are at the office holiday party (see page 62), limit yourself to one or two drinks. But not wine. Wine is for people who don't drink.

Suggested Drinks: Keep a decanter of good bourbon (not Scotch—too cliché) in your office with a few glasses. Deploy this at strategic times with employees who will carry the message of your beneficence and charm back to the rest of the company.

Drinking and Working in Your Yard

Unlike office work, yard work is often *not* done for pay, but instead is forced upon people by the burden of homeownership. In these cases, you cannot be fired from your job, and so adding alcohol to it is less of a risk. You'd be surprised by how terribly (or infrequently) you can mow a lawn before anyone mentions anything.

The trick, as mentioned before, is knowing which work can be done terribly—and with relative safety—and which requires precision or threatens injury or death if done while under the influence of twenty beers.

Drinking Allowed During Outdoor Housework

LEVEL OF INEBRIATION	TYPES OF WORK ALLOWED
Not inebriated at all	• Anything that requires an open blade, like a saw or those pruning shears that look pretty much designed to remove fingers • Roof-based work, like shingling or gutter-ing • Stone wall or path construction (if you are the stone-placement decider) • Basically anything requiring tools that need to be plugged in
Slightly inebriated—e.g. if required, you could read aloud in a church or other sobering place without worry	• Ladder-based work (above three steps) • Hammer-and-nail work, including but not limited to deck-building • Painting • Mowing, snow-blowing, and other work with machines that shut off automatically when you take your hands off them
Normal inebriated—e.g., you all of a sudden have a lot of stories you wish to tell those around you	• Shoveling work—both snow and dirt • Most gardening activities • Anything involving a wheelbarrow • Pool cleaning (assuming you can swim of course) • Stone wall or path construction (if you are the stone-placer)
Really inebriated—e.g., when asked, you actually cannot name all of your children. Some of them? Sure. But all of them? Pssssshhhh.	• Most leaf-based work, including blowing, bagging, and pile-making • Weeding (this actually requires being really inebriated) • Lugging • Anything involving the mythical two-wheeled-barrow • Garage-cleaning

Service Work

All service workers may consume as much alcohol as they wish in order to get through their shift. If you have ever worked *one* shift in the service industry—bartending, retail, waiting tables, cooking, hotel desk monitoring, et al.—you will not question the soundness of this advice.

Drinking and Artwork

When it comes to drinking and artwork, you have two approaches. You may ask yourself: What kind of art am I trying to create? And then find the alcohol that will encourage you in that direction. *Or* you may start from the booze end of things: What and how much booze am I about to drink? And then find the art that would best complement your boozing. Both are successful and have been used by generations of artists in the production of creative work.

Refer to the table on the next page to find the right liquor/art pairing for your current state.

ALCOHOL	CREATIVE WORK	EXAMPLES OF SUCCESSFUL CREATIVE PRODUCTS
Bourbon whiskey—and lots of it. Glass optional.	Stories about the American South in which the memory of the Civil War plays a major part and children must deal with the sins of their parents. And also, ghosts may very well be real.	*As I Lay Dying* by William Faulkner
Bloody Marys interspersed with daiquiris or similar citrusy cocktail	Stories about men and their adventures, in which the adventures seem romantic. Upon reflection, though, the men are actually monsters, and there is no meaning to anything.	*For Whom the Bell Tolls* by Ernest Hemingway
Five or more gin martinis	Witty, sparkling social satire with weak characters and kind of obvious plot	*The Portable Dorothy Parker* by Dorothy Parker
Fifteen or more beers	Chaotic, abstract work made by throwing one type of material at another type of material and hoping something sticks	*No. 5, 1948* by Jackson Pollock
Mint juleps interspersed with hard drugs	Work made by cutting up existing stuff and remixing it into something basically incoherent and disturbed	*Naked Lunch* by William S. Burroughs
Marijuana interspersed with mint juleps (replace muddled mint with muddled marijuana)	Work made by cutting up existing stuff and remixing it into something basically better than the original, or at least funnier	Any piece of music that comes up when you Google "Awesome mash-ups of '80s songs and '90s hip-hop"

ALCOHOL	CREATIVE WORK	EXAMPLES OF SUCCESSFUL CREATIVE PRODUCTS
Rum and coffee followed by rum and Coke	Story about a loner who fights crime alongside a reluctant talking vehicle of some type	*Knight Rider* by Glen A. Larson
Bottle of wine (sherry)	Knitting-based work	*Two Kittens In the Grass* by Grandma Miller, Dayton, Ohio
Bottle of wine (red)	Crocheting-based work	*Riot Grrrl Manifesto in Threads* by the Slutty Needle Bitches, Portland, Oregon
Whiskey and malt liquor	Stories that romanticize youth and travel and jazz narrated by and starring some real dicks	*On the Road* by Jack Kerouac
Scotch and waters	Stories about wealthy people and how cold they are and how weird their sexual desires are	*Rabbit Is Rich* by John Updike
Four bottles of wine	Brechtian allegory of corruption and corporate greed that includes very thinly veiled portrayals of capitalist fat cats and is set in a place with a name like "Workerville, USA"	*The Cradle Will Rock*, directed by Orson Welles
All the liquor currently available to you	Bluesy, guitar-driven rock and roll mostly about sex, appropriate for humongous stadiums	"(I Can't Get No) Satisfaction" by the Rolling Stones

For many people, college will be the first time they encounter liquor, at least in the mostly unrestricted way of an American adult. Sadly, these encounters are mostly disgusting and about as far away from proper drinking as you can get.

Combine that with the fact that these young adults are also basically unsupervised and around a bunch of peers who are also experiencing first-time unrestricted access to booze; and then combine *that* with the fact that they (or their parents) are spending a lot of money for them to be there *and also* that they are basically setting the course for, if not the rest of their lives, then at least their twenties, and you have probably the worst idea ever. Who thought this would work?

Learning how to drink at college is the first real test you will have of self-regulation around booze, and thus it is important to be on your guard, lest you get the wrong idea about things. To aid you in this, please review the following list of fallacies about drinking.

Some *TOTALLY FALSE IDEAS* You May Have About Drinking if You Learned About Drinking *IN COLLEGE*

- Most alcohol is consumed from red plastic cups.

- Parties involving alcohol should take place in the grossest houses possible.

- Kegs are EVERYWHERE and good for doing gymnastics on.

- SoCo and root beer is a good combination.

- Serving liquor from a garbage can is a great idea.

- Most drinking involves a weird game with Ping-Pong balls that isn't fun.

- That guy who graduated but still hangs out at college parties? Yeah, he's a cool guy.

- It's fun when losing means being forced to drink health-risk levels of liquor.

- Drinking is always best when done at the fastest possible rate.

- Boots, blocks of ice, funnels, and human belly buttons are perfectly normal and acceptable vessels for alcohol.

- When drinking, you should dance like a stripper.

- The best way to buy alcohol is in the largest quantity possible for the least money possible.

- Cuervo Tequila is good.

- Most bars require that you stand outside in a line wearing way too few clothes and possibly even shower sandals.

- Many bars will honor your meal-plan card.

- Eating a burrito AND a falafel at 2 a.m. is a good idea.

- People's lawns are good places for sleeping.

- Shots and highballs are the only way to drink spirits.

- Being drunk means you get to shout at things. Especially inanimate things.

None of the above is true! Any reader of this manual should understand that drinking can be done with grace and with proper glassware. In order to shield oneself from the bad habits of college drinking, it is recommended that you follow these basic rules:

- Never drink (or buy) liquor from plastic bottles.

- Don't drink anything that lists food coloring as an ingredient.

- Drink more wine than beer.

- And (sadly this must be said) never ever take advantage of someone who is drunk. A Drinker always protects those around him or her, *especially* the very drunk.

The only exception to the fourth rule is when encouraging drunk people to do karaoke, which is less a matter of taking advantage of them and more like helping them realize their full potential.

What Is Allowed?
And What to Do About It!

In most states, you are not allowed to drink alcohol in public. There is no *federal* law about this, so it is up to the states to decide whether it's cool or not, and most states agree: It is not cool. They decree this in what are called "open container laws," i.e., laws that control not whether you can drink in public, but whether you can have an open container of alcohol in public, the idea being probably that you don't want your hard-working police force to have to deal with some jerk holding an open vodka bottle going, "Yeah, but did you see me drink from it?"

But of course, people drink in public all the time. The fact that you can even buy a flask reveals the existence of this behavior—just like head shops and Phish concerts are a weird legal symbol of a lot of illegal weed smoking and jam band music listening.

So even though the law in most states is very clear, the reality of public drinking is much more varied. It breaks down to three basic types:

- Totally legal

- Sneaking it where it's illegal

- The Authorities-Look-the-Other-Way Scenario

The Totally Legal

Only seven states in the United States allow open containers in public—Georgia, Louisiana, Missouri, Montana, Nevada, and Pennsylvania—which really means they don't actively ban it. Instead, they pass the buck onto their municipalities to dictate whether and how their citizens might imbibe publicly. New Orleans is probably the most well-known example, but other cities allow it and are even more permissive than the Big Easy. In New Orleans, for instance, the open container law states that you are only allowed to carry booze around in the French Quarter, and only in a plastic container. (And while there is no actual law about it, as far as I can tell, you are also required to drink your unholy French Quarter liquor through a twisty straw). Same goes for Savannah: plastic container, under sixteen ounces, only in the Historic District.

In Butte, Montana, however, there are no restrictions whatsoever to drinking in public. The lack of federal law filters right on down to your individual freedom. It's the only city in America like that. Glass container, a forty-ounce Negroni, wherever the hell you want—in Butte, drinking alcohol is a public right.

THE EXPERIENCE

While in some ways, these open-container cities seem like a public Drinker's dream come true, there is something manufactured about the experience, like being at a theme park for drinking. This can be fun, but if my experiences in New Orleans and Savannah are any indication, it feels a little juvenile.

Rather than "drinking in public," this type of imbibing feels more like drinking in a giant outdoor bar. Which, nothing against giant outdoor bars (obviously), but it is still a licensed environment—thus the rules about plastic cups and cops patrolling the party. Legally drinking on the street in New Orleans feels like legally drinking in a bar anywhere else in the world, except with shittier drinks (con) and more unsolicited boobs (pro).

THE PERFECT DRINK

What goes in plastic and tastes good through a straw? *Frozen blended drinks*. If you have to drink it like a Slurpee, it might as well be in Slurpee form.

Sneaking It Where It's Illegal

On the other end of the open-container spectrum is where you find the good old flask, along with its less elegant, more economical cousin: the water bottle filled with vodka.

Now we're getting into it. Both the flask and the water bottle are ways to sneak alcohol in areas where open containers are not allowed; and both have their pros and cons.

I own a cheap, unmonogrammed, six-ounce, stainless-steel flask, which is to say: I didn't get my flask as a groomsman gift. My flask epiphany came when I realized that along with convenience-store candy, I could also sneak whiskey into my local movie theater. No single realization has improved my life more than this, reader! (For more on drinking in movie theaters, see page 80.)

THE EXPERIENCE

Or so I thought. The flask looks cool, but it's a totally terrible method of actually sneaking alcohol anywhere. The flask just showcases that you are trying to hide alcohol; it's as if you attempted to sneak bullets by hiding them inside a gun. Everyone knows what's in there, Humphrey Bogart.

Which makes using a flask kind of awkward and adds a patina of shame to your coolness. Even in a darkened movie theater, people will recognize the weird pursed-lip-and-quick-wrist-tilt the flask requires of you. You may as well just shout to those around you, "Hey, there! I have snuck alcohol in here!"

The water bottle filled with Bacardi 151 is much, much sneakier, but this is not to say it also doesn't have it's downside. You may fool more people, but associating your drinking with fooling people is never something you want to strive for. So, personally, I use a flask and accept what may come. if you are going to sneak alcohol somewhere, you may as well be open about it.

THE PERFECT DRINK

Whiskey, whiskey, whiskey. No question, right? And it's got to be some good bootleg whiskey. The flask is already a symbol of prohibition, so go ahead and complete the costume.

Also: To be clear, never, ever put alcohol in a water bottle and pretend that it is water.

The Authorities-Look-the-Other-Way Scenario

Between the two poles of totally legal open containers and sneaking alcohol into public spaces lies the great sweet spot of public drinking: drinking in such a way that isn't tricking anybody, but isn't causing any hassle and so the authorities just look the other way. Drinking in public parks on a sunny Sunday is a good example of this.

The beer bottle in a brown paper bag best symbolizes this compromise and its central truth: a lot of public drinking isn't worth busting. I remind you of Major Howard "Bunny" Colvin's great observation from *The Wire* about the brown paper bag, in which he calls it "a great moment of civic compromise. That small, wrinkled-ass paper bag allowed the corner boys to have their drink in peace. And it gave us permission to do police work."

Of course, the compromise hinges on the integrity of the public Drinker to not do anything that would require police work—acting belligerent, peeing against a building, doing a bad Sylvester Stallone impression. The paper bag won't prevent you from becoming a drunk asshole, in other words.

THE EXPERIENCE

Unlike the flask, the paper bag seems a more agreeable way to announce you are sneaking alcohol.

Maybe it's because the paper bag has no flash to it. Rather than shouting to everyone around that "Hey, I am drinking hooch here! And I own a pocket watch!" the paper bag is understated. "I won't bother you, if you don't bother me," it seems to say.

THE PERFECT DRINK

Beer, usually. It fits great inside a brown paper bag and doesn't telegraph trouble in the same way hard liquor in public can.

That being said, there are those scenarios—like at a drive-in movie theater or a secluded park—where wine and/or gin and tonics are definitely the way to go.[8]

8   Assuming you aren't driving of course.

Five Ways to Fill a Flask

||||||||||||||||||||||||||||||||||||||||||||||||||||||||||||||||

1. Straight and sloppy

2. With a funnel

3. First pour into
   a measuring cup
   with a spout

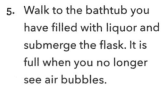

4. Mama-bird style—first pour
   into your mouth, then put
   your lips to the flask, and
   expel the booze into the flask.

5. Walk to the bathtub you
   have filled with liquor and
   submerge the flask. It is
   full when you no longer
   see air bubbles.

Going on a First Date

So you are on a first date! Congratulations!

Alongside selecting your outfit and making sure you don't have spinach in your teeth, choosing your drink can be one of the most important aspects of a first date. It helps set the mood and establish your personality, and can be called upon to smooth over any awkwardness.

To properly deploy alcohol on your first date, you consider three things:

1. Choose a drinking style appropriate to how well you know the person.

2. Choose a drinking style that showcases the vibe you want to give off.

3. Avoid and/or handle date emergencies with the correct drinking maneuver.

With those three pieces in place, you will surely have success.

FIRST CONSIDERATION:
HOW WELL DO YOU KNOW YOUR DATE?

We have been friends for a while.

Challenge: This is the easiest situation to predict and plan for. If you have been friends for a while, you most likely have drunk alcohol with him or her before. Your date may have even already seen you inebriated. It's also possible you made out at a party while inebriated and are now going out for a first date.

For the date, you may want to employ—or deploy—alcohol to foster a more-than-friends feeling, but you must be careful when doing this! Many first dates have been taken down by a poorly timed bottle of champagne. You wouldn't propose marriage on a first date, would you? So why would you order champagne and freak everyone out?

Drinking Strategy: Choose a drinking establishment that has a laid-back romantic vibe. Avoid candles, tablecloths, places with multiple wine glasses on the table. Avoid dinner entirely, I say. Look for something outside, preferably overlooking water. A rooftop bar could work, but again: Be careful it doesn't feel capital-*R* Romantic. This is important: Get the same drink and just keep ordering it. Don't make those drinks beer. If it must be wine, order it by the bottle. Mojitos or other laid-back cocktails would be just about perfect.

And then go home and let your hands wander.

Not that well. We've met once or twice and exchanged numbers.

Challenge: You need to confirm that the early flirtation and number exchanging were a good idea.

Drinking Strategy: Order your absolute favorite drink and see how your date reacts. Nothing showcases a Drinker's personality better than his or her favorite drink.

Not well. But I know a lot about him or her from the Internet, including our match percentage.

Challenge: All right, Drinkers, be careful. While Internet dating has been truly wonderful for many, many people, it presents a whole new kind of problem: thinking you know the person better than you actually do. Before the year 2000 you wouldn't have gone on a first date having seen multiple pictures of someone; or having a very good idea of the kind of books your date likes; or knowing your date's feelings on shellfish; and/or being aware at all of the most private thing your date is willing to share.[9] The Internet provides a false sense of closeness that can cause Drinkers to let down their guard. Even if your match percentage is high, remember, you kinda lied on *your* online dating profile, so . . . you know . . .

Drinking Strategy: Just as the Internet can make you feel overly familiar with someone, drinking can make you not care how familiar you are with that someone. It is a dangerous combination. Internet dating must be handled with caution by Drinkers.

9   Of course, yes, there are cases of pen pals falling in love over letters . . . Oh wait: NO, THERE ARE NOT.

Start slowly, and don't be overly familiar about what your date may like or doesn't like vis-à-vis drinks. Order one drink and hold off on the second one until you answer the question: Do I want to stay here, or do I want to leave?

If done correctly, a Drinker can expect that the slow and steady application of alcohol will allow the cold, false (but also probably weirdly accurate) computerized compatibility to blossom into actual human, flushed-cheek compatibility. Think of the alcohol as the water to the seed of algorithmic connection.

You know nothing in advance. This is truly a blind date.

Challenge: A quick and clear understanding of whether this is going to work.

Drinking Strategy: Ask if you can bring your date a drink. If the response is, "No, I'm all right," then go to the bar and order a shot of whiskey. Drink it, and then leave.

If your date says, "Yeah, bring me a . . ." then bring it and see how it goes.

SECOND CONSIDERATION: WHAT KIND OF VIBE ARE YOU TRYING TO GIVE OFF?

Next choose the drink that will help you project the vibe you are going for. Like your outfit, your drink choice gives off a strong first impression, so make sure it is the impression you want to make.

VIBE	DRINKING STRATEGY
Funny and fun!*	Order the most bizarre thing on the menu, and acknowledge it as the most bizarre thing on the menu.
Active and adventurous	For reasons unclear to even our most clever scientists, outdoorsy types (those who enjoy pursuits like outdoor walking, rock biking, and whatever "kayaking" is) like to drink beer from Vermont or Oregon. So you should drink beer from Vermont or Oregon.
Mysterious and haunted	The mysterious and haunted types should order a whiskey neat and then spike their own drinks with MORE WHISKEY they brought in a flask.

* **Warning:** A lot of people trying to be funny and fun end up ordering drinks that are wacky and sad, like a Sex on the Beach. Don't do this. The more crazy a drink's *name*, the less crazy it actually *is*. Instead, go for the one with the most number of ingredients or the most ingredients you are unfamiliar with.

VIBE	DRINKING STRATEGY
Sophisticated and hard to impress	Order a classic cocktail that everyone has heard of (what good is sophistication if no one knows you are sophisticated?)—like a sidecar—and then leave it unfinished after one sip and a slight, *slight* grimace.
Down-to-earth and dog-owning	A glass of red wine. When you drink it, say: "I don't know much about wine! I just know what I like, you know?" or "Tastes good to me! I mean, it's red, and it's wine, right?!" And then laugh in a noticeably practiced way.
Dumb and easy	Simple mixed drinks with no more than four syllables—Jack and Coke, vodka and Sprite, rum and OJ, Amaretto and—lots of them.
Timid	Don't order until asked directly, then say: "Whatever *you're* having." Blush.
Dungeons and Dragons-ey	Mead and Cherry Dr Pepper.

THIRD CONSIDERATION:
HANDLING SPECIFIC DATE SCENARIOS
WITH SPECIFIC DRINK MANEUVERS.

The above strategies form the foundation of your first date. Below are ways to handle specific situations that may arise. Simply layer them atop the foundation, and the date will be delivered safely to its correct conclusion.

Your date is boring you.

Be gracious and continue to ask questions. A Drinker is always gracious and always asks questions. It is one night out of your life. If you know this is going nowhere, buy more drinks and enjoy your evening.

You are boring your date.

If you realize you are boring your date, you are already miles ahead of most boring people. Use that awareness to *stop being boring*. Stop your story, say, "You know what? I am boring myself, here." Then ask: "Have you ever had absinthe?" You will immediately cease being boring *forever*.

Your date asks your opinion about a topic with which you are unfamiliar.

Drinkers never pretend to be something they are not. If asked directly about something you have no real knowledge of—the political intricacies of the Israeli-Palestinian relationship, say, or Stanley Kubrick's early work—don't feign knowledge. Instead, pick up your drink, hold it in front of you, and say, "I actually don't know much about that. What should I know?" And then take a sip while keeping eye contact. The sip communicates that you are done speaking; the sip plus eye contact communicates *this is a good conversation, and I find you interesting*.

NOTE: A Drinker always strives to find the other person interesting.

You just did something embarrassing.

If it was not drink-related: Smile, accept it, apologize, wave self-deprecatingly if others are clapping. Go back to sipping your drink. *Sipping* will show that you are in at least some control.

If it *was* drink-related, you don't care, do you?

You tell what you think is a funny story, and it falls totally flat.

The worst thing you can do in this situation is take a sip from your drink during the silence. It will only punctuate the silence following your dumb story. Instead, utilize the technique made famous during the 1990s alt-comedy boom: Fill the silence with a meta-joke about your bad joke. Something simple like, "Note to self: Never tell that story again," while pretending to write on a reporter's notepad. With the silence broken, quickly follow up with, "I'm going to get another drink, you want one?" Regardless of whether your date wants one, or whether you even need one, go to the bar. This will cause a natural transition and give you time to think of a question to ask. When you return with the drinks, ask your question immediately—put the ball in your date's court.

You are told that you remind your date of his or her mother or father.

Ask what his or her mother or father drank, and then order that.

How to Throw a Drink in Someone's Face

IIIIIIIIIIIIIIIIIIIIIIIIIIIIIIIIIIIIIIIIIIIIIIIIIIIIIIIIIIIIIIIIIIIIIIIIIIIIIIIIIIIIIIIIIIIIIIIIIIIIIIIIIIIIIIIIIIIIIIIIIIIIIIII

As previously discussed, Drinkers primarily use alcohol by ingesting it through their mouths. However, throwing a drink *into* someone's face is also a totally legitimate way to use alcohol *if the situation calls for it*. It communicates to the other person that he or she has crossed a line and can go no further in your presence. It is less violent than slapping someone, and more stylish. You have emptied your drink. You are done.

That being said, throwing your drink in someone's face should be done only as a last resort, when all your other drinking resources have been exhausted. In order to be justified, throwing a drink in someone's face must first be preceded by:

- A review of the nearest exit

- A look of shock

- A shaking of your head while you stare at your drink

- A verbal warning, such as "take that back" or "whoa, whoa—that's not right"; let the other person know you will not accept his or her statement or actions

If none of these three "warning shots" are heeded, a Drinker has no other choice but to empty a drink into the other person's face.

But of course, to be successful, you have to actually get the liquid from your glass onto the other person, a skill not as easy as it looks in the movies. Successfully "Throwing Drink," as it is called in the industry, requires a quick and fluid wrist as well as good aim. The motion also depends on the type of glassware you are packing and whether the drink contains ice or not.

Proper Drink-Throwing Technique

Step 1—The Grip

You want a solid grip—a Drinker never throws the glass, just its contents—but not one that tips off the other person that you are getting ready to cover him or her in booze.

Step 2—The Visualization

Every good drink thrower knows that success happens first in the mind. Imagine your drink crossing the empty air between you and your prey; imagine it as an extension of your arm, arcing like lightning across the sky.

Step 3—The Lunge

A mistake many first-time drink throwers make is starting from the wrist. This will not generate the amount of momentum required to get the drink across the table. Start from the shoulder, and then extend your arm and wrist like you're cracking a whip.

Step 4—The Retraction

Just as quickly as the glass shot forward, pull it back. You want to displace *all* the liquid in your glass in one movement so that it doesn't fall short and slosh uselessly to the table.

Step 5—The Stand and Pivot

This move is a matter of personal style. Some drink throwers like to toss out a good quip as they walk out—"You pig" or "Your views are old-fashioned, and now you're covered in one"—while others simply let the drink throw do the talking. Either way, pivot on your heel quickly and head to the door. If you can find someone to high-five on the way out, all the better.

It is totally acceptable to toss a drink in someone's face if he or she:

- acts mean to a child (who is apparently in the bar?)

- insults you with the intention to harm

- insults anyone in the bar with intention to harm and/or is making others feel shitty

- asks you to throw a drink in his or her face because it is "kind of my thing"

- needs to snap out of it!

- needs to be woken up and the normal shoulder shake isn't working

- claims that *The Watchmen* movie is way better than *The Watchmen* graphic novel

- their hands go somewhere they should not go

- performs slam poetry on a date with you

Breakups

Breakups are like the wipeouts of the emotional world. People don't start skateboarding because they want to fall down; they start because they want to do all those cool, flippy things. Similarly, people don't start relationships with breaking up in mind—they start because they want to do cool, flippy things *in bed*. In most cases, though, a breakup is inevitable. As a species we have not figured out a better method for partnering up than good old trial and error. And it's mostly error.

Like skateboard falls, breakups can run the gamut of pain. On one end of the spectrum, a relationship ends, and you feel elated. It's the best thing that ever happened to you. On the other end, your life is shattered, and you are staring into some serious, black-hole infinity shit. In the middle, you are sad and listen to Phil Collins records. And you drink.

Drinking during a breakup is both important and risky. This goes for drinking during any sort of emotional pain, I suppose. Drinking does wonders for emotional pain, though; it is like the codeine of the emotional pain world. It can slow down your thinking and block some bad-thinking patterns. It can get you closer to the pain in some cases, and further away from it in others. It can help you deal.

It can also seriously fuck you up and turn you into an emotional train wreck with the maturity of a teenager.

The key to avoiding further fucked-up-ness is understanding what type of breakup you are going through and then applying the correct drinking technique. It's like homeopathy, except that it actually works and will make you way more fun at parties.

There are three major types of breakups, each causing a different level of pain:

- If you feel that a weight has been lifted, this equals a *low-pain breakup.*

- If you feel super sad, but life is still basically the same, you are experiencing a medium-pain breakup.

- If you feel that your whole life is fucked up in a real and dramatic way, then you have just gone though a serious-pain breakup.

- There's a corresponding drinking strategy for each of these types of breakups:

LOW-PAIN BREAKUPS

Drinking strategy: Get some action and party.

Garden variety, it's-not-working-out breakup (you are the dumper)

Also called the "it's not you, it's me" breakup.

Don't be an asshole, here. Yeah, yeah, you were the one who ended things, and you are super happy to be done with it, but this isn't the time to go out and hook up with three people in one night and rub the other person's face in it.

This is like buying a handgun—you must wait at least two weeks before pulling any sort of trigger on someone else. OK, maybe one week.

So, first week: Invite people over to your house and drink a bottle of wine—you can have a whole bottle to yourself, whatever, I don't care—but do not go out. Repeat: DO NOT GO OUT.

Second week: Let the reins out.

Relationship naturally, mutually came to an end

This is the most rational of breakups. It could be that you are moving to different cities, or graduating college, or you are enlightened French people who never assumed this would be a lifetime thing anyway, and isn't love so mysterious and beautiful? Regardless, these breakups present a combination of freedom with a measured, wistful sadness unique to adults who know to reserve epic sadness for events involving death and sports teams.

Assuming it isn't weird for your friends and you aren't lying to yourself about the other person's pain, you are allowed to go out and have some good old-fashioned, young-person fun. Go to a club and order party drinks like tequila shots and other shameful drinks you never thought you would need/get to do again. But it's important that you balance those nights out with a few evenings of reflective after-dinner drinks (Dubonnet would work, or cognac, of course) taken on the porch or somewhere where you can stare silently into the distance and toast to your ex, who deserves it.

MEDIUM-PAIN BREAKUPS

Drinking strategy: Dramatic wallowing.

Garden variety, it's-not-working-out breakup (you are the dumped)

So, you didn't want this relationship to end, but the other person did. Sorry, that sucks. Let me buy you a beer.

See what I did, there? Let me introduce you to the "social wallow drink." I am assuming you have been dumped before, so just have your friends take you out and get you full-on hammered. For good measure, trash-talk your ex. It will hurt the next day, but at least the hurt will put your breakup hurt into perspective. The hangover? That's real pain.[10] You'll get over your ex.

You keep breaking up and getting back together, and your friends are sick of it

Your friends are no longer offering social wallow drinks, but it would be pitiful if you went off by yourself to drink absinthe and write poetry. In fact—you do not get to drink. You need to look at yourself in the mirror and make a few sober-faced decisions.

SERIOUS-PAIN BREAKUPS

Drinking strategy: Measured, and in the company of friends.

Hmmm, I don't quite know what to say about this one. This is maybe a don't-drink situation. You are volatile on a whole new level. If you get out-of-your-head wasted, you might do something crazy.

Drink only under supervision. This is a powder-keg situation, and to be honest you should be, like, going to yoga and getting all calm and figuring out how to move on from your anger. This can super easily turn into one of those "I'll show him" sort of situations. Booze will only get you there more quickly.

But OK, if you must, you may as well do it up right: a bottle of Jack Daniel's gripped around the neck, ready to walk over to their house and make your case from the street. To accomplish this, invite some friends over who can supervise a glorious

10   See Dealing with Hangovers, Page 124.

fuck-you session with your bottle of whiskey; and then ensure that they have the authority to tackle you to the ground when you actually do try to leave the house to plead with or curse out your ex.

Long-term relationship in which lives are intertwined

Damn, there is nothing to celebrate or be needlessly dramatic about here. This is truly sad. You need to go out with good friends, not for a bitch fest about your ex, but for a life-affirming, it's-always-darkest-before-the-dawn sort of rally.

Go out, but not for a rager; get dressed up, but not in order to pick people up. Go and get a really amazing cocktail, made with precision and care in a nice, quiet bar. There is a perfect buzz that comes on after one martini—a buzz in which the world is not swaying, but is actually a tad crisper and all of a sudden inherently joyful. That is what you are shooting for. Don't over-shoot it—stick to the one.

Charles Baudelaire wrote that liquor causes "an inordinate poetic evolvement" in us. We're not talking about the poetry of the teenage drama queen. This is the "adult real shit" poetry in which life slows down, narrows to the room you are in, and allows you to focus on what is important and beautiful and continual. Shit will continue to be pretty awful for a while, but remember that there is also this feeling; even now, this feeling.

DEALING WITH HANGOVERS

Look: There is no cure for your hangover. Sorry. You drank too much and had three pieces of cake (or whatever), and you didn't drink water, and you took a shot of Jameson right before leaving the party. No magic potion will fix that. You deserve the punishment meted out by the morning light (and its awful, awful cacophonies).

Hangovers follow the immutable laws of the universe: For every action, there is an equal and horrifying sensitivity to light. While hangovers are evil, we need them; for, they keep the world in balance. You can't have Superman without kryptonite.

Even though we know this—just as we know we shouldn't have had those five champagne cocktails—we will always try a crazy cure, anything, anything to Make. This. Stop.

So we will stumble to the medicine cabinet—or to the gym, or to a brunch place with Bloody Marys—and do our best to beat the unbeatable.

You can tell a lot about a person by which hangover cure he or she clings to. There are two kinds of people: those who attempt to head their hangover off at the pass, and those who don't. It's actually a little tough to say which is the more responsible group. Sure, the preemptive hangover fighters prepare and plan (responsible), but they are planning on drinking too much (not responsible).

Planning Ahead

The following strategies are to be employed either before or during your drinking session. For the real go-getters, try all of them at once, though a more scientific approach would be to try one at a time, see if any make a dent in the next morning's headache.

MODERATION

On the responsible end, this is the only guaranteed hangover stopper: not drinking too much.

To those of you who are able to successfully practice moderation, I say: Good for you. Now would you please wipe that "I told you so" grin off your face while the rest of us wallow in our shameful headaches? Thank you.

WATER IN BETWEEN EACH DRINK

This responsible hangover-fighting technique combines the drinking style of the prehangover glory days—ah, to be twenty-two again—with the problem-solving skills of a full-grown adult human. As the Internet will tell you, drinking water during a binge accomplishes two helpful things:

- Combats the dehydrating effects of booze.
- Slows your dumb ass down.

Those who choose this route know the hangover well—only those who've been down this road before would choose to drink that much water—but they also refuse to stop their hangover-inducing drinking. Instead, they have evolved and cultivated a sober voice *within* their drunken brain. It's like having a nagging spouse with you at all times—"Don't forget to drink water!"—which, in this case (as in many others), will keep you from drinking even more than you would have.

EATING A BIG MEAL OR TAKING A SPOONFUL OF OLIVE OIL BEFORE DRINKING

See the water method, above. This is basically the same. Thinking ahead and trying to trick your body into thinking you aren't drinking *that* much.

That being said, if you *are* taking a spoonful of olive oil before drinking, at least look at yourself in the mirror while doing it. You need to own up to what is happening right now.

PRELOADING WITH VITAMINS OR SOME CRAZY PILLS WITH NAMES LIKE "SHOOTER" OR "CHASER"

This method is interesting because the Drinkers who employ it have decided to put their faith and well-being in the modern equivalent of snake oil.

While wonderfully hopeful, those who rely on this pre-remedy are actually dangerous to others and whatever nice furniture you have at your party. Thinking they are magically avoiding the consequences of getting wasted, they can sometimes cross over into "I'm invincible" territory. Remember all that stuff about hangovers keeping the world in balance? Yeah, this is why.

And yet: You need to fly too close to the sun at least once in your life, so I say give the snake oil a chance if you haven't before.

Dealing with Your Hangover After the Fact

All right, so now that you have a hangover (I told you those pills wouldn't work), how are you going to handle yourself? While science says that none of the following methods will actually work, you will probably give anything a try, right? Anything to make this stop.

EATING GREASY FOOD (MOST ESPECIALLY EGGS)

Apparently there is something in eggs that counteracts the poison in your body. Whatever. I am sure there are other nonbreakfast foods that can do the job even better. You choose this technique not for the chemical composition of eggs, but because brunch is awesome. All good nights deserve a good morning, which is why this remedy is best for groups of hungover people. What's almost as fun as drinking champagne with your friends? Having brunch with them!

Subnote to this: I am told some people advocate the eating of burnt toast. I am fine with this, but refer to the spoonful of olive oil on and ask yourself, "Am I really about to burn toast *on purpose* because I am idiot?" If the answer is "yes," then go for it.

HAIR OF THE DOG

Eventually, on every hero's journey, he or she realizes that the only way out is through. You can't slay a dragon by replenishing electrolytes.

The hair of the dog has been around as long as hangovers—indeed, many of our most precious cocktails (the zombie, the corpse reviver, all of the fizzes, and basically anything with bitters in it) were first conceived as hangover potions. Who cares about science (which says it won't work, by the way)? The hair of the dog is a tried-and-true method simply because rather than fighting the hangover, it is a complete surrender. The Bloody Mary is basically a white flag to the monster.

(Sidenote: There should totally be a cocktail called The White Flag, which is not a dumb layered shot.)

Anyone who reaches for the bottle the next morning is either:

A. A varsity-level Drinker, possibly someone who works in the bar trade and so uses "more alcohol" to cure lots of stuff.

B. An idiot college student who is using it as an excuse to drink beer at 10 a.m.

C. In the throes of the worst hangover ever, and holy hell, he or she will try anything.

Remember, though: when you make a deal with the devil, you eventually pay something awful.

PAIN PILLS

The old standby and the cure most often adopted by weekday Drinkers. Pain pills will not work if you are hung over in a deep and fundamental way, so it is best for people who can manage to say peppy things about their hangover like, "I'm actually a little hungover this morning!" or "Whew, I had quite a night last night!"

EXERCISE

Really? Are you sure you are hungover?

Apparently this is a thing some people swear by. This is for those who actually don't drink to excess that often. It is a way for some Drinkers to prove to themselves that they are not who they were last night. No, no, they go for runs and stuff.

Unlike the hair of the dog or a pain pill, hangover exercise is a form of self-punishment. It's like a parent promising a principal: "Oh, his mom and I will make sure Bobby is adequately reprimanded for drinking that whole bottle of wine."

LYING ON THE COUCH, MOANING

Denial and wallowing won't heal you, but sometimes they are your only option. This is the gateway cure to hair of the dog.

Most hangover cures are about distracting yourself or your body from how crappy you feel. This one indulges in it. In a way, it is similar to the exercise method, but with a touch of shame. Exercisers prove to themselves that they are not as debauched as they behaved last night; moaner/sleepers, on the other hand, just ask themselves over and over, "Why?"

SHOWERS (EITHER HOT OR COLD)

Showering is the least you could do and something you should do anyway, so don't pretend this is a cure.

BURYING YOURSELF IN SAND UP TO YOUR HEAD, OR HUFFING SMOKE FROM A FIRE

I am not kidding. These are both documented hangover cures. I've never done either of them, nor have I known anyone who has attempted them, so I can only speculate on the type of person that deals with a hangover in this way. I get the sense that whoever came up with these cures was drunk at the time. It would take a lot of work to bury yourself in the sand or build a fire while hung over, though, so whoever would do this is probably pretty industrious.

Part III:
BUILDING A BETTER DRINK CULTURE

THE ETIQUETTE OF DRINKING WITH OTHERS

Regardless of event or role, there are a few guidelines for successfully drinking with others. The Drinker loves company and should be loved by that company. To be a positive element in a group, a Drinker should become expert at buying drinks for others, introducing and guiding others to new alcohol, and giving and participating in toasts.

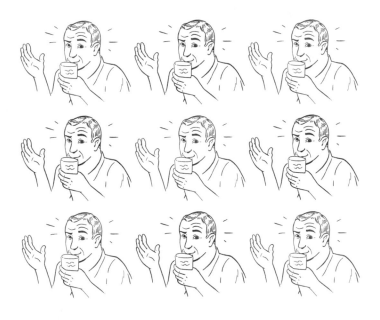

YOU SUCK AT DRINKING

When to Buy the Next Round

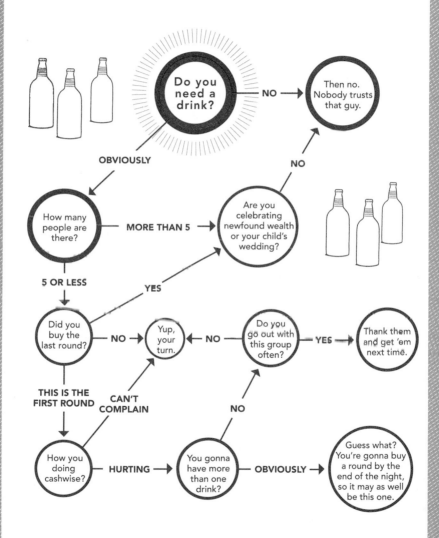

Introducing Others to New Alcohol

As a Drinker, it is your duty to spread good drinking within your community and to introduce others to alcohol they may be missing out on. When you have the chance, always try to introduce others to alcohol they have not tried.

But be precise with your introductions. Changing drinking habits is a delicate process that shouldn't be rushed. If a Drinker were to bring out all the tools and specialized equipment required for a proper absinthe tasting too early, a normal person might reasonably think drinking were a strange cult or a kinky pastime.

Instead, use the following role-play scenarios as a guide to properly introduce others to new-to-them alcohol:

SCENARIO 1

A Drinker meets a new friend for drinks. The new friend orders a vodka cranberry. The Drinker knows this is a dumb drink. What should the Drinker do?

A) Nothing. A person's drink is a person's drink.

B) Laugh immediately and with meanness in your heart. Vodka cranberry is for losers.

C) Secretly tell the bartender to make this friend the Benton's Old-Fashioned from Jim Meehan's *The PDT Cocktail Book*. And then, when the bartender looks at you weird, say, "What? You haven't *heard of it*?"

D) Order a citrusy cocktail, like the Hemingway daiquiri, and then tell your friend you made a mistake in your order and offer it to them. "I meant to order a traditional daiquiri," you can say. "You should have this one."

SCENARIO 2

A Drinker is hosting a small party. She knows that at least one of the guests is a self-professed Beer Drinker. What should she serve?

A) Beer, of course! One must always serve what people think they want.

B) Make a pitcher of Michelada, a cocktail made of beer, lime juice, and various salty and spicy sauces normally reserved for steak.

C) Make a pitcher of daiquiris or other citrus-heavy cocktail palatable to most people, and hide all the beer in the garage.

D) Spend all day muddling strawberries and mint for a delicious summery cocktail with light rum and lime juice and sparkling water. Put it out on the bar next to a bottle of bourbon and then watch as no one drinks the summery cocktail—watch as all the ice melts and the mint gets waterlogged and the strawberries begin to resemble entrails—because hey, there's bourbon.

SCENARIO 3

A Drinker is at a cocktail bar with a friend. That friend says, "You're into cocktails. What should I get?" and hands you the menu. Well? What should the friend get?

A) Whatever you are getting. It will show confidence in your choice.

B) Ask what the friend likes, and don't accept "I don't know" as an answer. "Come on," you can say, "are you into spirit-heavy drinks? Or do you like lighter stuff like fizzes or cobblers? I've been really into punches lately, but I doubt they make their own oleo-saccharum here . . . hmmm. I'd love to introduce you to rye that is bottled in bond. How do you feel about overproofed spirits?" When your friend answers all your questions, you will be much better able to choose something.

C) A sidecar.

D) Shake your head and mouth the words "Whoa" while turning away.

The Answers

Scenario 1: **D.** Noncoercive or secret recommendation is one of a Drinker's best tools.

Scenario 2: **Trick question.** As a Drinker, you will probably serve all of the above and more.

Scenario 3: **C.** The sidecar has never missed. It nails the landing every time.

How to Cheers

Though we are a pretty loose culture when it comes to social etiquette and rules, formality still finds places to hide itself. Raising a glass of liquor and saying "cheers" has a long history—so long we don't really know the origin—yet it remains a standard and nearly universal way to begin a drinking session or meal. It is one of the things that separates captial-*D* Drinking from other activities and substances.

And yet, like a lot of remnants from old formal culture, cheers-ing can create confusion and awkwardness in social settings. We aren't sure which rules to follow because there are so many different rules; and their application is unclear to say the least.

TOASTING TODAY: COMMON TOASTING SCENARIOS AND HOW TO HANDLE THEM

Along with many bygones of drinking culture, Prohibition dashed formal toasting upon the rocks. Nowadays, the long-winded, formalized elegy is reserved mostly for weddings and for hanging out with Eastern Europeans. In its place is the quick raise of the glass along with, more often than not, a noncommittal "Well . . . cheers everyone." Most will clink glasses; someone will demand eye contact; people sitting far apart will awkwardly stretch or, more horribly, shuffle around the table to make sure they clink with everyone. It can be an unsuccessful mess. Just because we have lost the speeches doesn't mean we can't take full advantage of the moment. Here then are some suggestions for when and how to properly cheers.

YOU SUCK AT DRINKING

TYPE OF TOAST	FOCUS OF THE TOAST	PROPER TECHNIQUE	PROPER WORDS	COMMON OCCASIONS FOR THIS TOAST
The guest of honor	The guest of honor, obviously. During this toast, you are speaking on behalf of the group about a person you (presumably) all know.	Standing is appropriate unless the group is particularly small and can fit around one table.	This is the closest any of us will get to a celebrity roast, so take advantage and make fun of the guest of honor.	Weddings, retirement parties, birthday parties
Real friends	Often performed at reunions, or any time when you are with a group of people you haven't seen in a while, but holy crap, it's good to see them. Here you are speaking to the group as a whole.	Eye contact makes sense here, as does clinking. This is an honoring of everyone in the group and their connection to each other.	You know how you never can tell people how you really feel and one day we will all be dead and you'll be sad that you never told people how you really felt? This is your chance. Tell them.	Reunions of any type, holiday gatherings, you are straight up Big Chillin'
A holiday	Holiday toasts often come preloaded with themes and emotions you should be feeling and honoring. Thanksgiving calls for you to be thankful; New Year's gives you time to reflect on the past year and to make promises for the new one; July 4th celebrates grilling, etc.	As these are often meal-based toasts, I suggest a round-robin here that lasts throughout dinner, everyone giving small speeches on the theme at hand. No clinking or eye contact necessary. Just raise your glass in acknowledgment of what each person says.	"On this day, it's important to remember . . ." and then fill in holiday-appropriate remembrance.	Any holiday

TYPE OF TOAST	FOCUS OF THE TOAST	PROPER TECHNIQUE	PROPER WORDS	COMMON OCCASIONS FOR THIS TOAST
Just out for drinks	Nothing special, that's the point. This is like the dimming of the lights that signals the beginning of the show, or the bell that begins yoga class. It's a nice pause in your day, a "Hey guys, we are here together."	Raise your glass, lower your eyes, and then get on with your drinking. If the group is small enough, do a group clink, all glasses coming together like the album cover of Pearl Jam's *Ten*.	Any of the common cheers words; *cheers*, of course, but you can definitely throw in a non-English version: *Prost*, or *Skol*, or *Kassai*. Be careful using a non-English word, though, if you just spent time in that country. You'll sound like someone who always drops hints about being abroad. Worse than that, you will actually *be* one of those people.	After-work drinks, Weekend drinks, Lunch drinks, BBQ drinks, Drinks for no reason whatsoever
A dinner party	Usually a nice way to thank the hosts who just made you a fantastic meal	Raised glass	A simple thank-you will suffice, though you could easily incorporate the technique from Mark Twain's time: State something you wish blessings upon—the Boston Red Sox, for instance—and then bless them—"May their bats be swift and their curve balls curvy." That sort of thing.	Dinner parties (obviously)

SOME GENERAL TOASTING GUIDELINES

- Clinking in a group of more than five is ridiculous.

- Eye contact is intense. Do you really want your cheers-ing to be intense? If so, go ahead.

- When in doubt, cheers to everyone's health. It's like a little black dress or an old-fashioned—timeless.

- Doing the toast at a wedding is fraught with baggage and cultural expectations that you will be drunk and inappropriate. Don't let that happen to you. Practice your toast in advance.

- Go with the flow. If everyone is clinking, then clink. If eye contact is happening, so be it. But if it's not, then for god's sake, don't force it. Your job during the cheers is to participate.

The Glass-Drain

This is the mic drop of the drinking world. It must be accompanied by appropriate words; otherwise, it will seem too dramatic. Don't just say, "Well. . . cheers, everyone," and then drain your glass. That will worry people. Instead, pull this out at extreme moments that deserve it, e.g. when you are about to ask a stranger to dance *and you never dance.*

The Two-Person Armlock

Usually reserved for bride-and-groom-type situations, when the toast is also some sort of binding agreement. I've only seen this pulled off a few times in non-marriage situations, and it required that Italians be present.

The Multi-sip

For long toasts, you may want to split your words into chapters, taking a drink at the end of each one. Eastern Europeans excel here. The challenge here is to (a) know when the natural chapters are and (b) keep the attention of the group as they keep downing drinks at your request.

The Silent Salute

No words, just a raise of the glass. Very rare. This is like the Godfather of cheers-ing, requiring that you hold power and influence in the room and that your every action will be noticed and followed.

The Virtual

An emoji-based cheers. Choose the martini glass or the beer mug icon and send it at the right moment to indicate, "I am raising a glass to you now."

The Pick-Up

Cousin to the Silent Salute, this is a gesture employed when buying a stranger a drink. When the bartender points you out, raise your glass. Be careful not to overdo it.

The Homey Pour-Out

An evolution of the cheers in which liquor is poured out on the ground for someone who is no longer with us. Now often done ironically by bros in honor of their bro who just got engaged and so "is gone for good."

THE IMPORTANCE OF DRINKING AND PRACTICING GOOD DRINKCRAFT

And now I speak to you from the heart. The purpose of this book is to create a class of Drinker best suited to handle the realities and challenges of modern life. It is filled with the what and the how, but so far I have avoided the why. Now I make a case for *why* this knowledge and these skills are important.

Being a good Drinker is about more than knowing what to drink and when; or even how to handle oneself when intoxicated. The reason we learn and practice these things is so that when the time comes—when we head to the bar after work, or drink with our parents, or fill up our flask—we will feel comfortable and alive in drink's inherent irrationality.

Drinking, like all other drugs, transforms us into something slightly different than the sober brain we were born with. Sober brain creates skyscrapers and time sheets; drunk brain creates music and gloriously bad sex. Sober brain goes to work and deals with the mortgage; drunk brain tells stories and gambles away savings. Sober brain wants to keep you healthy and alive; drunk brain, making little sense, wants to burn you out in a glorious flash of sadness and joy.

The actual divisions between sober and drunk behavior are not so well defined, of course—sober people can have bad sex and write poetry, just as drunk ones can write a mortgage check—but it is always one borrowing from the other; the regions themselves remain as Nietzsche left them: Order and Chaos; Apollo and Dionysis; Knowledge and Wine. We are raised to feel comfortable amid the first, but not the second.

People find their way, some better than others, and drinking remains—as it always has and as it always will—a major part of our lives.

But many are lost when they get there. Chaos is called chaos for a reason, and when a person raised on order and skyscrapers wakes the next morning after a night in murky waters, they feel regretful and hungover; eventually they grow out of it. Drinking was a phase. Drinking was that time in college, or that time in Vegas, or a very sad period when the chaos grew and took over their sober and ordered lives and dashed it upon the rocks. That can happen.

The importance of being a good Drinker is that it teaches us how to thrive in the chaotic and irrational parts of ourselves and the worlds we have created. Map any city by its bars, and you will map the part that wants life to be more than it is; the part that doesn't want to get up for work in the morning but wants to get on a bike and ride through a sprinkler; the part that cares only for what will happen in the next five minutes and wants those next five minutes to be really, really great. Drink is intoxicating not just because of chemistry, but also because it gives us that five-minute focus. In those five minutes, life is great, and all the shitty sober stuff—all the disappointment, all the forms, all the ill-fitting clothes and fears of tomorrow—all of that no longer matters.

That is not completely true, of course. The clothes and tomorrow *do* matter. We need both. And without the proper approach, we can get too intoxicated by the five-minute focus. The lessons contained in this book are what *allow* us to become intoxicated and come back. The lessons contained in this book, varied as they are, all come back to a single principle: Enjoy and be better at the messy stuff; for, the messy stuff is just as valuable as everything else, and the stigma against that stuff is harmful. Let it be a point of honor to waste time in a bar, be committed to karaoke, and know how to drown our sorrows, and through that make our world more friendly, more weird, and not more stiff or closed off because we have lived in it.

I hope to buy all of you a drink sometime soon. It would be my sincere pleasure. Thank you.

ACKNOWLEDGMENTS

I raise my glass to:

Danielle Svetcov, for guiding me through thick and thin;

Jennifer Kasius for the editorial eye and for coaching this rookie;

Joshua McDonnell for the look and feel;

Carl Wiens for the illustrations;

The whole crew at Running Press for the publishing know-how;

John Hodgman and Katherine Fletcher for lessons on martini-making-and-drinking;

David Rees for taking my phone calls about books;

Eli Horowitz and Christopher Monks for my first wine column;

Alan Sytsma for the editorial belief that led to this book;

Room 389 and Commonwealth in Oakland for providing great bars to both write and drink in;

Mikkel Svane and Toke Nygaard for bossing me around;

Chip Brantley for conversations over cocktails and skype;

Jim Meehan for PDT and everything It inspired;

Rob Baedaker for the nicest email I have ever received;

Kevin Cline for Not About Wine and whiskey with bitters;

Monica and Chris Latkiewicz for the continued and continual support;

Sarah Reid for the vows that included cocktails and coffee among other things.

Cheers.

APPENDIX

INEBRIATION LEVELS A DRINKER WILL EXPERIENCE

INEBRIATION
LEVEL .... EXPERIENCE

0 .... Not inebriated at all. You have had zero alcohol in the past twelve hours.

1 .... You could still drive but have zero desire to do karaoke. None of the effects of alcohol can be felt, except maybe a small release of tension.

2 .... The everyday buzz. The most common state of inebriation, during which a Drinker can easily carry on a conversation, do the mental calculations required to catch a train on time, and accomplish all but the most taxing of work tasks. Most people would not even know you had been drinking. The Drinker often spends a portion of every day at this level.

3 .... Also called the Ridge, or the Knife's Edge. This is the level that every drunk person attempts to hold on to but that is as fleeting as a good morning stretch. One more drink sends you to the other side; no more drinks and you sober up more quickly than you wish. Often, a Drinker will say or think during this level: "I feel good. Things are really good. Even ten minutes ago, I wasn't feeling so great, but now? Yeah, I am happy to be here." Words associated with this level: fuzzy, cotton, buzzed.

INEBRIATION
LEVEL .... EXPERIENCE

4 .... Inebriation Nirvana. You have lost yourself; you
have zero inhibitions, but you don't yet need to sit
down on the curb and throw up. Most of a Drinker's
"embarrassing" moments occur during this level—the
crazy dance moves, the aggressive flirtation, the dares
involving jumping from something tall. Memories
from this state will be blurred, and a hangover is
guaranteed.

5 .... In the state of blacking out. Slurred speech would
actually be an *achievement* here. You will remember
only the most fleeting of moments from this state, and
those moments will be horrific. Subjectively, this level
feels just like resting your head against the glass of a
taxi because it is cool and cool is good, but the motion
is not so good and you should probably ask the driver
to pull over, but you can barely maintain this train
of thought, so forming words that would be coherent
to any other human being seems basically out of the
question. Jesus, you want to die. You would prefer
death over this. Oh the glass is cool. Cool is good.
Whoa. It's morning. You slept in your clothes. Do you
have your wallet?

6 .... Hard to describe, for how can one describe the inside
of a black hole? The laws of gravity shift; what went
down now comes up; the pull downward becomes
impossible to resist, and you slide to whatever floor
will have you, spiraling into nothingness.

Below is a list of some of the physical and mental side effects of drinking. Drinkers should be aware of which sensations they are experiencing and how best to react to them.

SENSATION	DESCRIPTION	COURSE OF ACTION
Giddiness	The reason most people drink. Giddiness is a type of bubbly happiness, a self-reflective state of contentment.	Enjoy it.
Tingly brain	This is alcohol crossing the blood-brain barrier, also called The Great Wall of Tingle. This is the sensation that causes many folks to say, "Whoa, I'm actually a little drunk."	Stay the course, but start slowing your pace.
Warmth or flushing	As if your body were somehow glowing. Your cheeks feel like you've been sitting by the fire.	Do not mistake this for actual warmth and wander outside and take a nap in the snow. You are not actually warm, and that snow is actually very cold.
Sudden onset of loud voice	The moment you (or those around you) realize that you are talking really loudly.	Ask, "Whoa, am I talking really loudly?" And then laugh LOUDLY.
Slight egomania	You are washing your hands in the bathroom and catch yourself doing your "hey there" face in the mirror.	Don't indulge this. Laugh it off, finish washing your hands and say to yourself, "You are drunk, sir/madam . . ."

SENSATION	DESCRIPTION	COURSE OF ACTION
Fuzzy brain	You become aware that normal thinking has become harder.	Reduce the items (and the complexity of the items) on your mind. Switch your activity from adult conversation to something like watching an action movie or running around the backyard.
Foot too large	Also called "Arm too long." Your body hits something or knocks something over that it wouldn't normally hit or knock over. You stand there looking at it, confused at your size.	Stop staring at whatever you knocked over, as this will only make you look more drunk. Own your clumsiness, and then wrap your hands and feet in towels to make them less destructive.
Vibrating vision	While trying to sign the credit card receipt, it—the receipt that is—moves back and forth as if it were starring in a music video.	Close one eye and do your best to sign your name. Remember your card. Continue to an activity that allows you to lie on your back with your eyes closed.
"This isn't good."	A non-specific sense of unease that you recognize right away is "not good."	Probably throw up?
Heavy right side	You want to walk straight, but that right side is just so heavy.	Imagine that your left side is also really heavy.
Early-onset hangover	A dull headache that announces itself while you are still drunk; and what it announces is that you are going to be supremely hung over tomorrow.	Food, water, and then sleep quickly.
Room spin	The final stage before (hopefully) throwing up. Worse when you close your eyes. Feels like a roller coaster you are too old to be on.	Nothing you can do but wait and quietly moan and ask out loud: "Why?" in a long, drawn-out cry.

We are a nation of Drinkers, and yet regional differences do abound. Did you know that Zinfandel means different things to Northern Californians than it does to rural Georgians? It's true. When traveling across our great land, it can be challenging to communicate with those you meet in bars. To aid in cross-cultural drinking, it is important that you study the following official state terms for being drunk. It might just save your vacation!

STATE	OFFICIAL STATE TERM FOR BEING DRUNK [11]
Alabama	Ala-slammed
Alaska	Eaten by the Bear
Arizona	Lost in the Desert
Arkansas	Sober
California	Redwooded
Colorado	Rocky Mountain High
Connecticut	Undoing the Top Button
Delaware	Ratified
Florida	Spring Broke

11   That I made up

STATE	OFFICIAL STATE TERM FOR BEING DRUNK
Georgia	Punched by the Peach
Hawaii	Surfing the Big One
Idaho	Potato Headed
Illinois	At the Log Cabin
Indiana	Hoosiered
Iowa	Iowasted
Kansas	Lying in the Great Central Plain
Kentucky	Bluegrassed
Louisiana	Down in the Bayou
Maine	Clobstered
Maryland	Merry-land
Massachusetts	Fahking Wasted (Wicked Pissed is also acceptable)
Michigan	Stranded in the U.P.
Minnesota	Swimming in Lake Number 10,001
Mississippi	Miss is Sippy!
Missouri	Show Me, State!
Montana	Boozeman
Nebraska	Homesteaded
Nevada	Welcome to Fabulous Nevada!
New Hampshire	Miles to Go Before I Sleep
New Jersey	Hack and Sacked

STATE	OFFICIAL STATE TERM FOR BEING DRUNK
New Mexico	Shiprocked
New York	Huddled Mass
North Carolina	I'm Tarred and Heeled
North Dakota	**Previous:** Rough Ridden **Current:** Extracting from the Brakken
Ohio	Bucked in the Eye
Oklahoma	Okie-dokied
Oregon	Hanging out in Portland
Pennsylvania	Part of the Holy Experiment
Rhode Island	Spiking the Coffee Milk
South Carolina	Shagged!
South Dakota	Hanging in the Badlands
Tennessee	Walking in Memphis
Texas	Fighting Santa Anna
Utah	Golden Spiked
Vermont	Eat More Kale
Virginia	Visiting Monticello
Washington	Catching Some Sun
West Virginia	Strip Mined
Wisconsin	Happy Days
Wyoming	Going to West Dakota

If you find yourself in the past or the future, you will need to order a timeline-appropriate drink if you want to fit in. Consult this table on the next page for which drinks will help you blend in no matter when you end up! Note: some periods have multiple appropriate drinks.

TIME PERIOD	DRINK
9500 BC to 5000 BC	Wild-yeast-fermented sour beer imbued with spiritual powers
5000 BC to AD 800	Wild-yeast-fermented sour beer (nonspiritual)
6000 BC to present	Wine
9000 BC to AD 1600; or during a present-day Renaissance Fair	Mead
AD 1100 to present	Distilled spirits (neat)
1700s America; or 1900s Britain	Cider
1800–1920; 1995–present	Classic cocktails such as the sazerac, the martinez, and the sidecar
1950–95	Gross cocktails involving syrups, milk, crème de anything, and whipped cream
1950–present	Highballs
1973	Boxed wine
1990–present	Craft ale
2067–97	Laser wine
2050–2230	Dehydrated cocktails
1999; 2034–2400	Cocktails in a pill
2146–2147	Alcohol brain implants
3732–?	Cocktails involving star dust and dark matter

Drinks Consumed While Writing

Negroni. 104

Bloody Mary. 104

Gin Martini 52

Sazerac 13

Old Fashioned 52

Beer 78

Wine 5

Bourbon Neat 365

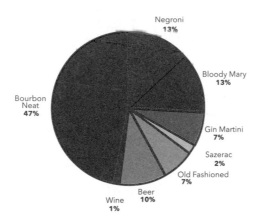

Contacting the Author for Drinking-Related Advice and Help

Our relationship need not end here! If you have questions about drinking and/or need advice during a drinking emergency not covered in this manual, please call or text the **Matthew Latkiewicz Drinking Hotline** at (510) 463-4520; or e-mail your NEEDS to matthew@youwillnotbelieve.us. All calls and e-mails will be thoughtfully considered and responded to!

Disclaimer: Any calls, texts, or e-mails may be published on the Internet in the way that a lot of advice columns work. Your question could help others!

INDEX